Empty Nest, Full Life is a [...]
the good, the bad, the fu [...] [...]ration, the decision-
making, the stress, and th[...] joy: Jill Savage writes truthfully and
vulnerably—and her readers are the recipients of powerful strategies
for turning the empty nest years into a season of rich opportunities
and purposeful living. Jill's advice—to give yourself grace, keep your
mouth shut, and to love no matter what—hit me smack-dab in the
heart! Buy this book for yourself, then gather your friends together for
a book study. I highly recommend it!

CAROL KENT, speaker and author, *When I Lay My Isaac Down*

Like having a cup of coffee with a trusted friend, Jill helps moms look
beyond the empty nest and into an exciting future. Just as a mom
cheers on her children when they spread their wings and fly, Jill cheers
on the empty nester to dust off her own wings and soar. *Empty Nest,
Full Life* is a must read for any mom who has waved goodbye and
wondered *what comes next.*

SHARON JAYNES, bestselling author of *Enough: Silencing the Lies That
Steal Your Confidence*

Mom, the REST of life can be the BEST of life—and Jill Savage shares
just HOW to make the most of life's second half!

PAM FARREL, author of 48 books, including bestselling *Men Are Like
Waffles, Women Are Like Spaghetti* and *10 Secrets of Living Smart, Savvy
and Strong*; codirector of Love-Wise

Jill is a faithful friend through every seasons of marriage and
motherhood. She graciously gathers women in pursuit of wisdom,
passing on what God is teaching her along the journey. This book is
no exception. Motherhood doesn't end when the kids leave the nest.
There are new griefs, joys, and challenges. Jill is a trusted guide in
navigating through it all!

JULI SLATTERY, founder of Authentic Intimacy

Is your adult child making decisions that are seriously stressing you out? As a new empty nest mom, I needed Jill's wisdom and practical advice to help me navigate what I'm letting go of and what I can look forward to in this new season of my life! Not only does she tackle the tough and sensitive topics that Christian moms truly need and are afraid to talk about, but Jill shares her experience with transparency, humility, and with a loud voice of hope! Let Jill be your guide, your friend, and most of all, allow her words deepen your hope and trust in God's plan for your adult child's life.

BARB ROOSE, speaker and author of *I'm Waiting, God: Finding Blessings in God's Delay* and *Winning the Worry Battle: Life Lessons from the Book of Joshua*

Empty Nest, Full Life will fill the hole in your heart that's been left empty when your child has left home. Jill has a compelling way of making you feel like she's sitting across the table from you, hot coffee in hand, reminding you in her sweet, gentle way that God has not forgotten you nor is life over, but instead has a great adventure planned for you with an incredible full life ahead! It's a must-read for anyone who has, or is, experiencing the empty nest. This book is going to help SO MANY women!

SHARI BRAENDEL, founder of Fashion Meets Faith and empty nest mom of four

Practical wisdom, "get after it" ideas, and encouragement galore, Jill Savage astutely provides women with exactly what we need to not just survive, but thrive, in the empty nest years! Navigating changing relationships will be a challenge no more. Your heart will sigh and your mind will be fully engaged as you learn to navigate, celebrate and embrace your Empty Nest, Full Life.

TRACEY EYSTER, founder and director of MomLifeToday.com, author of *Be The Mom*, and empty nest mom of two for five years

Praise from Your Everyday Empty Nest Moms

I love this book! Jill has put into words so many feelings I've had as my children have left the nest. I really enjoyed the how to "let go" and how to "grab hold" tips for transitioning into a new and exciting season of life! Well done!

ADDIE PLEW, empty nest mother of four

I loved this book and found it to be so helpful. In unpacking each topic, Jill shares relatable experiences from her personal life. She also includes journal prompts, which encouraged me to more deeply reflect on the ideas in this book. I recommend *Empty Nest, Full Life* to anyone who wants to navigate the empty nest years with grace and purpose.

DEB ALEXANDER, mom of two, recent empty-nester

In her down-to-earth style, Jill helps all of us in the empty nest season think about ways to be intentional and purposeful with our lives. Jill draws on her personal experience and relationship with God, and in this book you will find hope and encouragement to make this the best era ever!

BONNIE MILLER, empty-nester for over ten years and mom of two married daughters

This book will encourage you as you face the reality of an empty nest and offers insight into what you can make your life to be after the kids are gone. My favorite line from the book is "There may be an empty nest, but there's a full life to be experienced." Reading the book gave me hope that there is life after raising my family, and that I have much to look forward to.

LORRIE WICKUS, empty nest mom of three (soon to be four)

This book is a winner! Jill really understands the dilemmas of moms in transition from hands-on parenting to the empty nest. I highly recommend this for any mama trying to navigate this new stage in life. Even not-so-empty-nesters will find value in Jill's down-to-earth, practical application.

BETH HANSON, empty-nester of two, grandma of two

Empty Nest, Full Life will open your eyes and heart if you are facing or struggling with the empty nest. Jill uses her own life circumstances and the Word of God to help heal your heart. You won't be disappointed. I have applied several of her practical suggestions already!

TAMMY GEISELMAN, empty-nester of one

This book is a must-read for anyone who has children who have recently or will soon leave home. Jill's easy-to-read style of writing offers personal experiences from her own life as well as stories and examples from other women who have previously traveled this road. She provides thought-provoking concepts as well as ideas on how to make the transition to this new phase of life based on solid biblical principles.

DONNA WHITE, almost empty nest mom of three

This book filled a need in my life. It spoke close to my heart and was relatable in so many ways. It also encouraged me to pause, step back, and evaluate my thoughts related to grandparent "entitlement" moments. A must-read for anyone heading into or experiencing the empty nest phase of life.

TRINA COX, empty-nester mother of two, Gigi of one

EMPTY NEST, FULL LIFE

Discovering God's Best for Your Next

JILL SAVAGE

MOODY PUBLISHERS

CHICAGO

Some details have been changed to protect the privacy of individuals.

Published by arrangement with Transatlantic Literary Agency Inc.

Some of the content on pages 11–12, 26–28, 66–69, 79–80, 90 are also found in somewhat different form on the author's website. Please visit JillSavage.org.

Edited by Pamela J. Pugh
Interior design: Ragont Design
Cover design: Erik M. Peterson
Cover illustration of nest copyright © 2019 by Lana_Samcorp / Shutterstock (1202663446). All rights reserved.
Cover illustration of pennant banner copyright © 2019 by olegganko / Shutterstock (286936874). All rights reserved.
Author photo: Michael Gowin Photography

ISBN: 978-0-8024-1928-6

We hope you enjoy this book from Moody Publishers. Our goal is to provide high-quality, thought-provoking books and products that connect truth to your real needs and challenges. For more information on other books and products written and produced from a biblical perspective, go to www.moodypublishers.com or write to:

Moody Publishers
820 N. LaSalle Boulevard
Chicago, IL 60610

1 3 5 7 9 10 8 6 4 2

Printed in the United States of America

To my parents, Duane and Patsy Fleener.
Thank you for showing me what it looks like
to have an empty nest and a beautiful, full life!

CONTENTS

Dear Mama who is letting go,

I know it's hard. I know it feels like a part of you is walking out of the house.

It doesn't matter if you have a little kid heading off to kindergarten or you have a big kid heading off to college—giving them wings to fly is hard.

I know you're thinking of all the things you didn't teach them, all the crafts you didn't make, all the snacks you didn't serve, all the times you weren't patient, and all the moments you didn't listen as well as you should have.

I know you're feeling all those "feels" because every mom does in some way. She's hardest on herself, and when it's time to let them fly, the "should haves" seem to rise to the surface more than anything else.

Let me tell you, sweet friend, that you did well. You weren't perfect, but you did your best. Our kids need an imperfect role model because they are imperfect themselves. God used your imperfections to perfect you and your kids.

As you let go, send them off with a wave, and then take that arm just a little further back to give yourself a virtual pat on the back.

You've worked for this day. Your job has been to work yourself out of a job—whether that's for a few hours a day as you have one heading to school or whether this is the launch into adulthood.

Remember, you are a mom, but you are also a woman knit together by God with passion and purpose. You may have lost touch with that along the way, but it doesn't mean it's not there. You just have to find it again.

Now give them wings and watch them fly. You've done well and there's so much joy to be found in the next season!

GETTING STARTED: THE ROLLER COASTER OF EMOTIONS

We mamas are all about nest-building. Once the stick turned blue or the adoption papers were filed, most of us started getting ready for our new family member. We assemble the nursery, fill dresser drawers, start scrapbooking, and adjust nearly every aspect of our life for the realities of parenting.

For about twenty years, we work hard to create a full life and loving home for this child. We sign a million permission forms, help them study for just as many tests, watch a plethora of sporting events, and sit through more music recitals and choir concerts than we can count. We take them to youth group, church camp, dance lessons, and soccer games. We dry their tears, cheer them on, correct and encourage them. On top of all that, we keep them fed and clothed, which is no small feat considering how fast kids change and grow. We pour our lives into these kids and—THEN THEY HAVE THE NERVE TO GROW UP AND LEAVE HOME!

Our youngest and his then-soon-to-be wife chose a December 21 wedding date. He had graduated from college two weeks before and she would finish up her studies the following May. That ceremony sealed their commitment and officially launched my husband and me into the empty nest season of life.

I was fully embracing my newfound freedom when Christmas came a few days later and the new year rolled in. In fact, I basked in my new season of life from January through July. It was August that threw me completely for a loop.

I remember when it happened. I was sitting in our living room scrolling through Facebook. Everyone was talking about Back-to-School specials. They were sharing deals on notebooks, paper, markers, pens, and crayons. That's when it hit me. My getting-kids-ready-for-school days were definitely over.

The tears began to roll, and I silently said to myself, *I don't like this. Not one little bit.* I used to love getting the kids ready for school. I loved the rhythm of the school year and the summer break. And as I thought about it more, I realized that I loved being responsible, being needed, and feeling the sense of accomplishment and the fresh start that happened every August as the new school year started. Come on, I loved *mothering* in general!

Sure, there had been days I wanted to throw in the towel. There were days I wondered where it was that a mother could go to resign. Now I was missing some of the sweet parts of mothering. I had what felt like a *forced resignation* and I didn't like it one bit. I'm not the only one. One mom said it felt like a forced retirement with no celebration. So true!

Up until this point, we've been in charge of their life and we've been responsible for them. Now they're considered an adult and are expected to make their own decisions. How in the world does a parent make that kind of transition? Some kids are easy to launch and others . . . well, you might liken it to letting a toddler drive a car. What's a mama to do?

Welcome to the roller coaster of empty nest emotions! My guess is, you picked up this book because you've felt that sinking feeling in the pit of your stomach. Your life, like a roller coaster, is on its way up a steep hill, if not already at the top. You take a queasy peek right before you plunge down at breakneck speed, much faster than you care for. The winds of change smack you in the face as the emotional roller coaster twists, turns, and loops, taking you to sometimes unthinkable destinations.

One of many twists on the coaster—I felt relief for not being responsible daily for other people than myself, but *whoa!* do I miss taking care of the folks I love. Right after that, another twist! I love that our money now only has to support two people instead of seven, but *yow!* I loved providing my kids with the things they needed and wanted. These are the emotional loops of this roller coaster ride that cause me to sometimes say, "STOP THE RIDE! I WANT TO GET OFF!"

I'm sure I'm not the only one feeling this way, so what's a mama to do with all these crazy emotions? How does she get off the roller coaster, emotionally stabilize, and transition her thought process from something lost to something gained? A new opportunity? An encore to enjoy?

Struggling to sort through the emotional tsunami of the approaching empty nest, I opened my Bible for direction. I headed to the book of Ecclesiastes, remembering this is where we can find the "in everything there is a season" verses. I was certainly in a new season. I was not only on the verge of the empty nest, but I was already a nana. With the thirteen-year age span of our five kids, I became a grandmother before our younger children were even launched into adulthood.

This particular morning, I picked up *The Message* version of the Bible. I usually read the ESV (English Standard Version), but today I was inclined to pick up my Message Bible. I made my way to chapter 3, and it was verse 6 that stopped me in my tracks. Here's what it said: There is "a right time to hold on and another to let go." Those words HOLD ON and LET GO jumped right off the page to me and I whispered, *Lord, that's what I need to stop the roller coaster. I need to know what it is I need to hold on to and what it is I need to let go of. If those are clear to me, I think I might be able to move forward.*

That became the focus of my prayers as I rode the emotional roller coaster of this new, disorienting season of life. In each new situation I've faced, I've breathed the prayer, *What part of this situation do I need to hold on to and what part do You want me to let go of, Lord?* Over time, God began to give me clarity. Getting these concepts straight in my head revolutionized my thinking, freed me from unrealistic expectations, and gave me the vision for the full life still ahead of me.

The last eight years or so of my life, I've been doing important internal work that helped give me a secure footing for transition. I want to encourage you to do some of that work as well. Before we move forward and jump into the specifics of what we need to hold onto and let go of, let's lay a firm foundation for our thinking.

The Roller Coaster of Stinkin' Thinkin'

What goes on between our ears causes us more problems than most of us understand. There's very good reason the Bible tells us in 2 Corinthians 10:5 to "take captive every thought to make it obedient to Christ." Too often, however, we let our thoughts go out of control, fueling a wildfire of fear and anxiety, burning up every bit of life in its path. If we don't learn how to take control of our thoughts, we'll end up in a desolate mental wasteland without hope. We'll also end up on an emotional roller coaster we don't need to be riding. There are three ways our thoughts get out of whack: lens, lies, and liability. Let's take a look at each of these.

Lens

"We tend to see things not as *they* are, but as *we* are." That truth bomb was laid on me one afternoon by my friend Doris.

She was helping me sort through a relational issue with one of my ministry leaders.

I've thought about that statement so many times as I've considered the lens I'm looking at a situation through, or the lens one of my kids is looking through, or the lens someone I'm in conflict with might be looking through. Our lens is formed by our upbringing and our experiences. It's affected by our own preferences and biases. Nobel Peace Prize recipient Muhammad Yunus says, "We see things the way our minds have instructed our eyes to see."

It's important to understand that our lens may or may not tell us the truth. For instance, if you grew up in an environment of mistrust, you may read every difficult situation through the lens of mistrust. There may be no logical reason for you to mistrust the person standing in front of you, but if your mind subconsciously tells you, "you can't trust anyone," you'll consistently see people through the eyes of mistrust. This will cause unnecessary problems in your relationships.

Some lenses are mutually exclusive. For instance, you may see life through an optimistic lens or you may see it through a pessimistic lens. Some lenses layer on each other like seeing through both the lenses of gratitude and compassion. What does any of this have to do with the empty nest? A lot! Our lens is the perspective we see this new season through. If it's a lens of lack, we see only what we're missing. If it's a lens of abundance, we see new opportunities in front of us.

Some of us are still dragging around our stinkin' thinkin'

from our home of origin. That's right! You may be forty, fifty, or sixty-something, but unless you've done something to untangle yourself from your own parents' stinkin' thinkin,' you're still seeing life through that lens. If it's not a lens that's positive and helpful, it may be time to get a new prescription for your "life glasses." I know . . . you're not used to looking at yourself. You've focused the last twenty or thirty years on your kids' needs, but now's the time to focus on your own.

I did this myself several years ago. When Mark and I were in a season of marriage counseling, the counselor asked me a question I had never considered: "Jill, when was the lie that 'feelings don't matter' first planted into your heart? That's some stinkin' thinkin' right there," he challenged. One of the places of pain in our marriage was my lack of mercy and compassion. I was a "buck-up" wife and a "buck-up" mom. When life was hard, I saw it through the "buck-up" lens, which lacked empathy and compassion for myself and others. The "buck-up" lens tries to fix rather than feel. It comes in handy in business but doesn't serve us so well in relationships.

Diving headfirst into what drove my thoughts in this unhealthy direction was one of the best gifts I could give myself, my marriage, and my kids. Sure, I wish I'd done that internal work while I was still actively parenting, but I didn't have the time, the know-how, or even the awareness that my lens wasn't serving me well. Now I had the time and the awareness, and counseling gave me the know-how to make a much-needed change in my perspective. This is part of the full life experience God has for me and for you!

What if you could experience freedom from thinking that doesn't serve you well? What if you got serious about identifying the lens you see the world through and did something about whatever part of that is relationally and emotionally unhealthy? What if you didn't think of it as "too late" but rather "just in time" to make a difference in the second half of your marriage, or in your ability to have a healthy relationship with your adult kids, or to influence young lives as a grandparent, or for you to experience the freedom you long for?

I *know* the difference this can make, and I invite you to take a journey to get there too. Here are some questions to get you started thinking, maybe at first on your own and later, if you want, you can invite your spouse or a close friend to share what they see in you as it relates to these matters. Finally, if you haven't before and you feel it could be helpful, set up some sessions with a professional Christian counselor to dispose of the old lens and establish a new, healthier lens to view the world through in this encore season of life. Getting rid of your stinkin' thinkin' is one of the best gifts you can give yourself and your family!

Am I more prone to pessimism or optimism?

Do I tend to use passive-aggressive communication rather than honest, straightforward communication with others? (Hint: sometimes sarcasm is passive-aggressive.)

Am I more of a fixer than a feeler?

Do I struggle with shame and feeling "less than" others?

Do I feel like I'm never "enough"?

Do I work hard to "keep people happy"?

Am I prone to isolate rather than reach out to others?

Do I feel God must be disappointed in me?

Do I feel hopeless?

Do I wonder what I have to offer to the world now?

Am I struggling with my purpose?

Sorting through these questions will help you identify some of the places where your lens may not be telling you the truth. Go ahead, dig in, and pursue emotional health. It's an important part of your empty nest journey!

Lies

What do you say when you talk to yourself? Those words give us great insight to what we believe about ourselves.

"I'm such a dork."

"I don't ever get it right."

"I'm not a good friend."

"I could never do that!"

"I'm a screwup."

"I don't have anything to offer the world."

"I'm not needed."

The lens we see ourselves through is one of truth or lies. Our perspective is colored by both the false things we believe and the truth that frees us from these lies. Lies hold us back and keep us bound up; truth frees us to be fully who God created us to be.

Often, we're so familiar with the lies that have been a part of our thinking for many years, that we don't recognize them as lies at all. They've become self-fulfilling negative beliefs about ourselves. Tearing us down from the inside out, these lies keep us paralyzed in fear and hopelessness.

Lies are usually about our worth and value. They're also about how we believe others see us. They're about our abilities or inabilities. Lies use our failures to define us. They often produce shame, which isolates us and keeps us from the community God created for us to experience.

What does this have to do with the empty nest? A lot! Our lies will keep us from seeing what we have to offer the world. They will steal our joy and keep us lonely. Lies will leave us feeling insecure and defeated, unable to carry out our purpose. They are a tool of the enemy that keep us from being effective in this world.

How do we stop listening to the lies and believing them? We have to replace them with truth! Here are some common lies matched up with God's refuting truth. Snap a picture of this list or write down the lies/truth on index cards to keep them in front of you. Then when the lies creep into your thinking, you have a plan for changing your self-talk starting today.

SATAN'S LIES	GOD REPLIES
I could never do that!	"I can do all this through him who gives me strength." —Philippians 4:13
I'm not good enough.	I am good enough because the Holy Spirit empowers me. "You will receive power when the Holy Spirit comes on you." —Acts 1:8
I'm worthless.	I'm God's treasured possession. "The LORD has chosen you to be his treasured possession." —Deuteronomy 14:2b
I'm ugly . . . inside and outside.	I am God's masterpiece. "For we are God's handiwork, created in Christ Jesus to do good works, which God prepared in advance for us to do." —Ephesians 2:10
I would be happy if . . .	My joy comes from the Lord. "The LORD has done great things for us, and we are filled with joy." —Psalm 126:3 "The joy of the LORD is your strength." —Nehemiah 8:10

SATAN'S LIES	GOD REPLIES
I can't forgive myself.	I can forgive myself. "There is now no condemnation for those who are in Christ Jesus." —Romans 8:1
I can't forgive this person.	I can forgive because Christ has forgiven me. "Be kind and compassionate to one another, forgiving each other, just as in Christ God forgave you." —Ephesians 4:32
I can't _____.	I can because I'm a conqueror! "In all these things we are more than conquerors through him who loved us." —Romans 8:37
I feel hopeless.	There is hope in God! "And we know that in all things God works for the good of those who love him, who have been called according to his purpose." —Romans 8:28

SATAN'S LIES	GOD REPLIES
God doesn't love me.	"I am convinced that neither death nor life, neither angels nor demons, neither the present nor the future, not any powers, neither height nor depth, nor anything else in all creation, will be able to separate us from the love of God that is in Christ Jesus our Lord." —Romans 8:38–39
I'm not smart enough.	I "have the mind of Christ." —1 Corinthians 2:16b
I feel so rejected.	I have been chosen. "He chose us in him before the creation of the world." —Ephesians 1:4a
I'm afraid.	"Be strong and courageous. Do not be afraid; do not be discouraged, for the LORD your God will be with you wherever you go." —Joshua 1:9

Don't let any more lies steal your joy or diminish your value. Become an expert lie detector today. Once identified, start moving your head and heart from the lies to the truth that will set you free!

Liability

A liability is something that works to one's disadvantage. Being liable indicates probability that something is likely to happen. It also indicates responsibility. If we mis-assign responsibility to ourselves when it doesn't belong to us, we can consider ourselves liable for consequences that really belong to our child and his or her decision. For instance, if our child ends up in jail, we can begin to think of all the things we did wrong to cause this, rather than letting him or her bear the weight of their actions.

Misplaced liability also happens when we assign the wrong meaning to other people's actions or inactions. Remember the lens where we tend to see things not as *they* are but as *we* are? If we're insecure, we tend to wrongly assign our adult child's lack of communication to something we've done. If we're judgmental, we tend to wrongly assign our spouse's tendency to forget special dates to their lack of caring. We see things through our own experiences, history, temperament, personality, and family of upbringing perspective, and we determine what someone else means with their words or body language. *The problem is that the meaning we assign to it often isn't accurate.*

When that happens, we become offended when offense

wasn't even something the other person meant. Or we become defensive when we misread body language. Or we start an argument with a family member because we misunderstood what he or she meant with their words.

For years, my husband, Mark, did this with me. When I was strong in crisis and rarely expressed emotion or processed grief with him, he read it as "you don't need me." This was part of that "buck-up" mindset I mentioned earlier. It had everything to do with my tendency to believe feelings didn't matter and nothing to do with how I felt about Mark. However, he assigned liability to me that didn't belong there at all.

I can easily do this when Mark expresses apprehension about something. I read it as "unwilling to do something new" when the external processor in him is just expressing his thoughts or feelings about doing something new. He's not saying he's unwilling to do it, he's just talking through his feelings.

We can also do the same thing with body language. When someone is quiet, we can misread their quietness as a rejection of us. Or we wrongly assign meaning that they're angry with us when they're really just an internal processor who is simply thinking about something. One mom I know shared that she tended to misread quiet "because when I was young and my stepdad didn't talk to me, it usually meant he was angry. So I was assigning meaning to this same experience in my adulthood based on my childhood. The problem is that's not usually why my kids or husband are quiet at all and I'm assigning a wrong meaning to it!"

So what can we do about this bad habit most of us do at one time or another? We can ask our thoughts! What I mean is, when we ask our thoughts, we simply put what we're thinking on the table. For instance, that mom learned to say to a loved one, "When I was a child and my stepdad got silent, he was usually angry with me. You're quiet today, are you angry with me?" Or I might say to Mark, "You're expressing fear about doing this. Are you saying you don't want to do it, or are you just talking through your thoughts and feelings about it?" When we ask our thoughts, we take away the wrong assumptions and clarify what the other person is thinking, feeling, or communicating.

Go ahead and give it a try! You'll reduce conflict and increase communication! You'll also be better able to handle the empty nest transition better, because you won't overcomplicate relationships with issues that simply aren't there. Not only that, you'll also be able to get off an emotional roller coaster you don't need to be riding, leaving the past behind and looking to the future with vision and possibility!

What the Future Holds

It was my very first keynote message at a Hearts at Home conference. I asked the five thousand or so moms in the audience to pull out a piece of paper and plot out the timeline of their life. I wanted to cast a visual for them that there is life after raising kids. Although it's dependent on the age you became a mother and on the number of kids you have, most moms have somewhere around twenty years of life after raising kids before they hit retirement age. Maybe you were home during your children's growing-up years. Or maybe you worked for all or part of those years. Whatever your situation—and the nest won't likely empty all at once—your life will change when your kids leave home. However, that's not the end. It's the beginning of something new!

WOMAN MARRIED AT 22, 2 CHILDREN

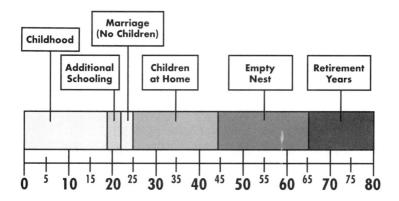

In my case, because I had a thirteen-year span between my oldest and youngest, I have about fifteen years of empty nest life.

JILL'S TIME LINE

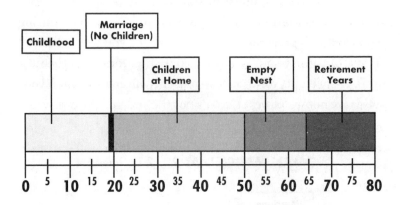

Go ahead and do this exercise yourself. How many empty nest years will you have?

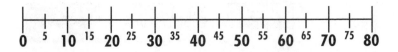

Most of us have (or had) a vision for our years of raising kids. We made decisions based on that vision and what we hoped to accomplish. However, that vision stopped after the kids were raised. What's your vision now? How do you want to intentionally use these encore years?

In just a page or two I'm going to give you some questions to ponder in an effort to help you find that vision. Word of warning, however—don't trip over into expectations. Vision leverages your wisdom, experiences, and passions to contribute to the world around you. It's a picture of what you have to offer the world as a whole, not just your adult children or grandchildren.

Vision captures the essence of who you are and what's important to you. If you think only about what you expect the empty nest years to look like, you'll likely end up disappointed because what you have to offer your kids and grandkids may not be appreciated or valued by them. You may end up disappointed because your reality won't look anything like your expectations.

However, if you'll focus on vision, you'll think outside the family box; you'll widen the playing field; and you'll leverage your wisdom, experiences, and passions to the bigger world out there. This is the value of vision.

So where do we start? How do we identify what we bring to this big, bold, beautiful world in this encore season of life? Let's start with a life audit. Pull out a journal, or a notebook, and start answering these questions:

Wisdom

What lessons have you learned about God over the years?

If you're married or were married, what lessons have you learned about marriage?

What have you learned about friendships?

If you could share hard-earned wisdom about parenting with your twentysomething self, what would it be?

How about self-care? What have you learned about self-care?

Experiences (fill in the blanks)

Growing up I experienced _____;
therefore, I understand _____

_____.

(unconditional love, an environment of encouragement, physical disability, an absent mother, an absent father, a compassionate parent, a critical parent, a parent with addiction issues, sexual abuse, an abusive parent, a passive parent, an angry parent, a buck-up parent, little family connection, a parent you had to "walk on eggshells" around, strong spiritual upbringing, no spiritual upbringing, a legalistic spiritual upbringing, mental health challenges, depression, anxiety, being adopted, and so on)

Our marriage experienced _____ ;
therefore, I understand _____

_____.

(pornography, infidelity, forgiveness, critical spirit, ADD/ ADHD, being spiritually unequally yoked, anger, abuse, passivity, physical health challenges, depression, anxiety, being a single parent, separation, divorce, navigating physical health issues of a child, loss of a child, and so on)

As a parent I have experienced _____;
therefore, I understand _____

_____

_____.

(a strong-willed child, a prodigal, adoption challenges, a child with mental health or physical health issues, a child with ADD/ ADHD, autism, same-sex attraction, a child who got pregnant or

who fathered a child outside of marriage, a child who is incarcerated, being a single parent, special needs, raising my grandchildren, loss of a child, miscarriage, infertility, C-section, breastfeeding challenges, and so on)

In life I have experienced _____;
therefore, I understand _____

_____

_____.

(loss of a parent, being in the caretaker role for a parent or an adult child with special needs, cancer, loss of a job, being a working mom, being a work-at-home mom, being a stay-at-home mom, postpartum depression, an eating disorder, depression, anxiety, abortion, overcoming a difficult upbringing, sexual harassment, betrayal, a broken friendship, managing a home business, being a volunteer, and so on)

Passions and Talents

More than anything, I want to see people _____

_____.

I get excited about _____

_____.

I'm passionate about helping moms/women/people/children _____

_____.

I can't help it, I just see the world through the lens of _____

_____

_____.

_____ comes naturally to me. It may be hard for other people, but it's easy for me.

People compliment me on _____
_____. I don't think it's a big deal but obviously other people do.

What did I put on hold when I started my family? _____
_____ Do I still have a passion or desire for that? _____
If so, what's standing in my way? _____
_____

If you have trouble identifying something you're passionate about, here are a few more questions to consider:

What do I enjoy? _____
_____

Is there something I do that really makes me feel alive?
_____

What gives me life? _____
_____

When I do this activity, I lose track of time: _____
_____

Do you see how much you have to offer the world? Your wisdom, your experiences, your passions and talents all make up the unique human being God created you to be. There's no one else like you. No one else with the same mix of lessons learned, life experiences, gifts, bents, and knowledge exists on this earth.

Your family may be the beneficiaries of all this experience and knowledge, but I want to expand your vision and remind you that others may benefit as well. You're a mother, a nurturer, a woman with a God-given design to impact the world around you. You have this season to shine. This is not a season of scarcity but one of abundance. As we launch into exploring what we need to hold onto and what we need to let go of, make sure you look at it all through the lens of abundance and possibility. This is the full life you're designed to have!

This Book Is for You!

I've done this five times . . . launching children into adulthood, that is. My husband and I have had the privilege of sending five kids into adulthood. They're 34, 32, 28, 25, and 23. Three boys and two girls. Three are married, and two of them have given us three school-aged grandkids. Life is full, crazy, wonderful, and sometimes hard . . . all at the same time!

It hasn't been easy, but it has been fulfilling. It's also been sad, exciting, disorienting, scary, and freeing. If you've felt any of those emotions, you're among friends.

Is the empty nest on the horizon? A little closer than you're ready for? This book is for you.

Are you in the throes of letting go? Trying to navigate a new normal? This book is for you.

Do you have some out of the nest and some still at home? This book is for you!

Is your nest empty, but you're still struggling to find the "full life" part of this journey? This book is for you.

As you turn the pages of this book, I will help you turn the pages of your life. This is a new chapter for sure, but you're still a mother. That will never change. Your kids still need you, but they need you in a different way. To be successful, you have to enter this new season of parenting with realistic expectations and I will help you do that.

You are not alone. On the pages of this book, you will find your tribe. You'll learn what's normal. You'll discover new opportunities available to you. Most importantly, you'll find out what you need to hold on to and what you'll need to let go of to experience the full life God has for you in this next season of motherhood. My arm is linked with yours . . . let's walk this together!

Part 1

LET GO!

"For I can do everything through Christ, who gives me strength."

Philippians 4:13 NLT

Chapter 1

LET GO OF EXPECTATIONS

I hadn't seen our youngest for several months. It was his freshman year of college and I was still adjusting to not being part of his everyday life. When he came home with his hair long enough to be pulled back into a "man bun" I was caught off guard. No longer was I privy to the decisions he made about his appearance. It may seem silly, but I felt left out.

Expectations will get us in trouble every time. They set us up for disappointment and leave us feeling disconnected. Being part of our kids' lives for nearly twenty years paves the way for certain expectations. We're accustomed to knowing specific things about their life and even chiming in on some of those things. However, when our kiddos leave the nest, those expectations have to change. With our direction from Ecclesiastes 3:6 that there's a time to hold on and a time to let go, let's take a look at four parenting expectations we need to let go of as we move into this new season of life.

Let go of expecting to know things

It was Jordan's first year at college. Attending school two hours from home, he and his parents were all adjusting to this new season of life. Jordan had played high school football, so his parents were accustomed to attending football games every Friday night throughout the fall. Even though Jordan was away and his parents had no one they knew playing on the team, they decided to go to the home game to keep up their tradition. As they settled into the bleachers, Dad snapped a picture of the team on the field and sent it to Jordon. *"Thinking of you tonight. Miss you,"* was the message he sent along with the picture. About twenty minutes later came Jordon's response. It was also a picture of the same football field with the message, *"LOL . . . I'm here too!"*

Mom and Dad weren't sure what to think. On one hand they were frustrated that their son had made a road trip home they didn't know about. On the other hand, they were relieved they actually knew where he was. And if they were really honest, they felt a little bit left out. Welcome to Reality 101 of empty-nesting: You have to let go of expecting to know things you would have known about in the past.

Your son or daughter is now making decisions independent of you. They're deciding how to spend their time apart from you. They're deciding how to spend their own money. They're making decisions about things you would have weighed in on in the past. Jordan's parents were in the middle of the muddle of empty nest transition. They decided to not make a mountain out of a molehill, but did ask that Jordan let them know when he would be making any major trips away from campus since the car he had on campus was theirs.

Sometimes it's not road trips but silly things like appearance that bother us. When my friend Marci's son sent a picture of himself and his girlfriend, Marci was so surprised her boy was sporting facial hair. Her son had never grown a beard before. This was new, and seeing the picture made him feel a bit unfamiliar to her. She admitted feeling a little left out of his life.

You and I have to let go of expecting to know things we used to know. We have to let go of expecting to be able to weigh in on their decisions. Of course, if they're going to school on your dime, you can still call the shots on some things, but if they're out on their own, paying their own way through life, you no longer have a vote. Even if you're still supporting them in some way, you still need to adjust your expectations to give them much-needed independence as they learn to spread their wings and fly.

Let go of expecting their priorities to be the same as yours

As our kids launch their own lives, they now have the freedom to determine their own priorities, too. You've laid the foundation for their life, but they get to determine what kind of house they'll build. I love what our pastor's wife, Sara, says.

"If they decide to build a shack on the foundation you laid for them, your job is to pray they'll eventually tear down the shack and build the beautiful castle you laid the foundation for."

Indeed, one of the hardest things to learn to let go of is determining their priorities for them. For nearly twenty years, you tried to help them make good decisions and set sound priorities. Now they need to do this on their own and it's entirely possible you won't agree with those priorities. This may happen gradually as they're entering adulthood and still under your roof, and it may happen when they're living on their own and starting their own family.

Several years ago, I coauthored the book *Got Teens?* with Pam Farrel. In our research, we found an interesting study concerning brain development. According to Dr. Jay Giedd at the National Institute of Mental Health, "the very last part of the brain to be pruned and shaped to its adult dimensions is the prefrontal cortex, home of the so-called executive functions—planning, setting priorities, organizing thoughts, suppressing impulses, weighing the consequences of one's actions. In other words, the final part of the brain to grow up is the part capable of deciding, I'll finish my homework, and take out the garbage, and then I'll [message] my friends about seeing a movie."[1] Studies indicate the brain isn't fully developed until the age of twenty-five. Yes, that means that our kids are now setting their own priorities when they're not actually fully equipped to do so.

Even without brain development being part of the picture, our young adults are simply different people than we are.

What's important to us may not be important to them, or it may take time for those priorities to kick in for them. For instance, family may not be a priority for them until they become parents themselves.

Our job is to give them the freedom to have different priorities and to resist the urge to shame or blame them for being different than we are. Our responsibility is to communicate the things that are important to us, but not to take it personally when our priorities clash with their priorities. This isn't the time to lament, "Where did we go wrong in raising this kid?" but rather staying steady with, "I know he's trying to figure out life and I'm going to give him the space and the grace to do so."

Let go of expecting them to communicate with you like you want them to

I have five young adult kids and they all communicate with me differently. Two of them I talk with almost daily. Either I call or text them or they call or text me. I know what's going on in their world most of the time. Child number three I hear from about once a week and number four and five I hear from about once a month. The pace of all those conversations is normal.

This is also true of their communication with their siblings. You may desire that your child has a close relationship with their siblings. However, they have to forge those adult relationships themselves. You laid the groundwork, but they will determine how much they'll invest as adults.

By the way, for most of us with more than one child, the

nest empties slowly. When the first child leaves, the supper table suddenly has an empty chair. You may be tempted to talk about the pain of that empty chair often, forgetting that the children who are still at home need you too. Be careful about sending an unintentional message to your kids still at home that they matter less by making frequent comments like, "I miss Madison so much; this house isn't the same anymore."

Every kid is different. Their need to connect with you and other family members varies as well. Some you'll only hear from when they need something. Others loop you into nearly every part of their life. Your job is to adjust to the pace they set.

You might be thinking, "Wait, how about my preference? What about my need to connect with my child?" Sure, you may want to communicate that you'd love to talk once a week, but if their desire is to connect once a month, you'll need to find a compromise that works for both of you. Your job is to communicate your desire directly ("I'd love to chat once a week") rather than indirectly in a passive-aggressive way ("I sure would love to hear from you more than once a year"). No guilt trips, no sarcastic comments, no underhand manipulating to get your way. Straightforward, honest communication surrounded with love and grace will give your changing relationship its best opportunity.

> Straightforward, honest communication surrounded with love and grace will give your changing relationship its best opportunity.

Let go of expecting to change them

Mamas are experts at seeing where our kids need to grow. We could identify it when they were under our roof and we can still see it after they move out and on with their life. Though we can keenly see changes that need to be made, the hard part is that we are no longer the authority to address the needed growth points unless they ask. If they ask, we can certainly offer our wisdom and share our concerns. If they don't ask, we need to keep our comments to ourselves, and commit our concerns to prayer.

My friend Becky says that when she's tempted to address something with her adult son, she tries to think of how she would address it with a friend. Most of the time she realizes she wouldn't address it with a friend at all! This helps her find self-control and pray instead.

Prayer isn't a second-rate option for us. In fact, it should be our first option. After all, God is far more powerful than either you or me! *Why, oh why do we get that turned around?* Our desire to control raises its head more often than we care to admit. Not only that but we try to force *our* timing. It comes down to trust: *Do I trust God to really put my children and their needed changes into His hands?*

This is also where we need to grieve what isn't and accept what is. If you raised your kids in a faith-filled home, but they've walked away from God, grieve that disappointment. Pour your broken heart out to God and then accept the reality that right now, you may be the only Jesus your child sees. Accept the reality that he or she is on his or her own journey of faith. Trust that God is pursuing them and loves them even more than you do. Pray and intercede for them each day.

Whatever the disappointment is, or the unhealthy parts of their life or relationships are, grieve what isn't that you wish was. Don't minimize it in your heart. Don't sweep it under the rug and not address the pain and disappointment. Shed tears. Admit the disappointment. Express your anger about this loss. Pour your feelings out to God. Once you've allowed grief to happen, move to acceptance. Ask for wisdom on how to be accepting of your child's reality. Remember, accepting isn't agreeing with. It's recognizing the reality of your child's struggles.

What is your disappointment with your adult child's life? What would you like to see changed but you know it's no longer something you can address? What do you need to grieve and then accept?

Change Your Expectations to Better Match Reality

Expectations get us in trouble in all our relationships. In fact, if we want to increase the joy in our life, we really need to stop having expectations of others. We can pray, dream, and hope, but not expect. We've focused on expectations as it relates to our adult children in this chapter. We can apply the same principles to expectations we have in marriage, with extended family, in our work environment, about our changing body, and more. In fact, we'll talk about most of those in the coming pages.

If we can learn to identify expectations and let go of them, we'll be better able to walk in love and grace. If we stop expecting to know things we would have known in the past, we'll be able to embrace something new when we see it. If we stop expecting our kids' priorities to be the same as ours, we won't be offended when our differences clash. If we stop expecting our kids to communicate as often as we would like, we'll better be able to appreciate the moments we get to connect with them. And if we will stop expecting to be able to change them, we'll be able to accept who they are and embrace the work God is doing in their life (even when it seems to not be at the speed we desire!). As you adjust your expectations to better match reality or let go of expectations of others completely, you'll find your contentment will increase, your love will expand, and your relationship with your imperfect kids will be strengthened.

Truth for Today:

"For I can do everything through Christ, who gives me strength."

Philippians 4:13 (NLT)

Take the Next Step:

Pay attention to your expectations (hint: they're usually revealed when you're experiencing disappointment or frustration). Begin to release others from your expectations so you can increase your sense of contentment and joy in this new season of life.

Talk with God:

Lord, I confess that I'm filled with expectations. Some are unrealistic, some unknown, and most are unspoken, but they're there. I know with Your help I can begin to let go of expectations so I can see the blessings right in front of my face. More than anything, may I always expect You to be at work in my life and in my kids' lives. In Jesus' name, amen.

Chapter 2

LET GO OF GUILT

I read an online article about talking to your kids about sex. It was an insightful article I forwarded to my daughter, a mother of an eight-year-old who is starting to ask more questions than her parents are comfortable with. As I pushed the "forward" button, a tinge of guilt came over me. *I sure do wish we would have handled the "sex" issue better when our kids were growing up. I would give anything for a do-over on that and, if I'm honest, a million other things!*

Hindsight is 20/20. We can always see things more clearly in the rearview mirror of life. That's because we can leverage both experience and context to see the situation with a more complete perspective. Then we were looking at the issue from the inside out. Now we're looking at it from the outside in. We're also distanced from the emotion of the moment, allowing us to not have our viewpoint skewed by the lens of emotion.

There will be things you wish you would have done differently—every parent experiences that to some degree! You and I have to let go of any guilt that wants to creep in and steal our joy. Let's take a look at how to do that.

The Accuser

"There is now no condemnation for those who are in Christ Jesus." That truth from Romans 8:1 reminds us that we are free from sin and death when we accept Jesus as our Savior. However, there is a battle for our head and heart that wages on. It's a battle between good and evil. Light and darkness. Truth and lies. John 10:10 (NLT) tells us, "The thief's purpose is to steal and kill and destroy. My purpose is to give them a rich and satisfying life." The Bible tells us Satan is the accuser (Rev. 12:10), and 1 Peter 5:8 tells us to "Be alert. . . .Your enemy the devil prowls around like a roaring lion looking for someone to devour."

If we don't understand this spiritual battle, we'll too easily succumb to the lies that are thrown our way. We'll believe the accusations and walk in shame and blame rather than freedom and grace. This will make us ineffective in relationships and powerless in faith. It will steal our joy, kill our relationships, and destroy our God-given purpose in this world. We can't allow that to happen.

So what's a mom to do? How does she deflect the accusations, stop the blame game, and turn guilt into grace and gratitude? Let's find some much-needed victory in that rear-view mirror.

The Perfection Infection

It was in *No More Perfect Moms* where I first introduced the concept of the Perfection Infection. The Perfection Infection is when we have unrealistic expectations of ourselves and when we unfairly compare ourselves to others. Stealing our joy and robbing us of contentment, the Perfection Infection heaps loads of guilt on our sometimes-fragile self-worth.

Social media can add to the Perfection Infection because there is a competition component in parenting when we see others' lives on social media. We have to remember their online photos are usually not showing us the hard parts of their lives. When I'm tempted to compare, I often say to myself, "She has a backstory I don't know." That simple reminder helps pull me back from the ledge of comparison and plants me on the firm foundation of reality.

There is no mother or father who parents perfectly. We're imperfect human beings doing our best to raise the next generation. We're still learning ourselves, and it feels like we learn some lessons too late to leverage them in our parenting. Indeed, we do. However, it's not too late to leverage them as a mentor, a mother-in-law, or a grandparent. It's also not too late to leverage them in our own lives.

I love the wisdom of Nelson Mandela who said, "I never lose.

I either win or learn." Over our twenty-plus years of parenting, you and I have a good number of parenting wins. We also have plenty of parenting "learns." If you have more than one child, you can leverage your "learns" along the parenting journey, but there's still no way you could ever get it all right. There's no perfection to be found on this side of heaven. I've found there are some important antidotes to the Perfection Infection. Let's take a look at these important keys to unlocking and throwing away mom-guilt that keeps us bound up in shame rather than free in authenticity.

Humility

I was at the end of my emotional rope one winter morning. It seemed every one of my kids and my husband were needy. There was nothing left of me to take care of one more need so in a less-than-kind response, the mommy monster showed up. I yelled in an effort to retain some sort of control. If I'm honest, the mommy monster showed up more times than I care to admit in the years I was raising my kids.

Do I wish I could go back and do it again and respond differently? Yep. Sure do. Can I go back and do it again? Nope. Sure can't, and neither can you. It's humility that allows us to adjust how we look at these less-than-ideal moments we *all* had.

If we don't deal with the guilt, it will fuel an unhealthy desire to "make up for" our mistakes. This isn't good for relationships at all. It keeps us feeling like we owe something to those we supposedly failed in some way. However, humility allows us to say, "We all make mistakes. None of us are perfect. I did my best and I've learned from my mistakes. I might owe someone an apology, but I don't owe them any more than that."

Believe it or not, guilt is actually a by-product of ego, and it's humility that helps us to put ego aside. "Humility" derives from a word that means "low or close to the ground." When we are close to the ground, that is, grounded, we aren't easily swayed. We stand firm in who we are, who we belong to, and who we are committed to be going forward. A grounded, humble person isn't looking for recognition because she is at peace with her worth in God's eyes. Humility helps us untangle ourselves from mom-guilt that tries to creep in.

Confidence

"Failures" can wreck our confidence. Turning these incidents into "learnings" will build confidence. Our "imperfect" seems to leak out entirely more often than we wish. As we look back over our years of parenting, the Perfection Infection operates as a magnifying glass of sorts. Our failures are magnified while our successes are minimized or even absent from our memories.

However, we can grow to assess ourselves through God's eyes, knowing it's His grace that overcomes where we have fallen short. His grace overcomes our imperfections, leading to a confidence that is aware of His purpose.

True confidence is really "God-confidence" or "God-fidence"

as I like to call it. It's not so much about believing in ourselves as it is about believing in what God did and does through us. It's learning not to repeat to ourselves the pointless "I can't" but to be assured that "God can!" Or as we think back, from "I didn't" to "God did."

I forgot my daughter Erica, not once, but twice in her childhood. I forgot to pick her up from an after-school practice and I forgot to pick her up from her gymnastics class one day. Both times I apologized and asked forgiveness for my mistake. God used those mistakes to teach my girl about apologies and forgiveness. That's an example of "I didn't" but "God did."

Erica struggled spiritually and emotionally in high school. In describing her struggles and how school and the youth group leaders at church handled her rebellion, she said, "Mom, there was a fire inside me. All they told me at church and at school was that I was 'making it smoky in here.' But you and Dad were trying to figure out what was causing the fire in me. You looked deeper." Parenting Erica wasn't easy, but this was a time we seemed to get it right. I'm sure there were other times she didn't notice or mention that we also got it right. Sure, plenty of mistakes, but also plenty of successes.

The antidote of confidence allows us to see how God led us, how He filled our gaps, and how He used our messes for His messages. Take your eyes off yourself and put them on God. Confidence allows us the freedom to embrace the imperfect human being we are, knowing that God is still at work in us and in our now-adult kids!

Grace

Our longing to handle life "perfectly" keeps us bound up trying. We tried to be the best mom we could be. We're trying now to be the best mom of young adults we can be. We try to convince ourselves that if we just work a little harder, we'll be more successful. Certainly, we need to do our best and pursue excellence, but perfection isn't possible and resting in grace is desperately needed.

When we deserve punishment but we get mercy instead, that's grace. Grace is at the core of our relationship with God. God's grace doesn't have to be earned. Instead, it is freely given. We just have to accept the gift of grace.

In human relationships, grace is allowing others to be human, to make mistakes and not get criticized for every little thing they do wrong or differently from the way we do it. Sometimes you and I waste so much time and energy nitpicking the littlest things that

> **What would happen if you said this to yourself the next time you remember a mistake? *I wasn't perfect, for sure. We all make mistakes, so I'm going to give myself grace and move on.***

our spouses, children, friends, and neighbors do. We jump to conclusions about people we do not know. What would our lives look like if we replaced judgment with grace? What freedom would we experience if we became grace-givers instead of judgment-makers? What if we started with ourselves?

Grace is a much-needed replacement for guilt. What would happen if you said this to yourself the next time you remember a mistake? *I wasn't perfect for sure. We all make mistakes, so I'm going to give myself grace and move on.* That's it; no beating yourself up, no replaying the incident over and over in your mind, no voice inside your head calling you names. Can you imagine the freedom you can have moving forward?

God sees us through eyes of grace. His message is, *Don't keep striving or living in your mistakes. Instead, live in My grace. I love you just as you are—no "perfection" necessary. Come find freedom first in an authentic relationship with Me and then in authentic relationships with others.*

Forgiveness

If there's one decision you and I need to make, it's the decision to forgive ourselves and others. In fact, grace requires a quick act of forgiveness. When we wish we had more time to "get it right" or think back to our "learnings" (remember, we're not going to call them failures), we may need to choose to forgive. The operative word here is *choose*. We won't feel like forgiving . . . we'll have to *choose* to let ourselves off the hook.

We're not perfect. We didn't have the knowledge to handle things differently then, so we're going to learn from it and move forward in our head and our heart. Looking at a situation from the rearview mirror perspective gives you a different lens and context than you had in the middle of the muddle. Understanding that will make the decision to forgive a little easier.

Forgiveness isn't one and done. We may stumble over that memory in the future, and if we do, we'll remind ourselves we're forgiven and we'll let forgiveness and grace wash over us afresh. We may also look at a situation from a different angle or outcome that causes guilt to creep back in. If that happens, we'll need to choose forgiveness once again. Our "learnings" are places where the enemy really wants to get in there and accuse, so we'll have to resist the temptation to take on any guilt thrown our way. When this happens, we'll have to actively choose forgiveness and grace instead.

Then there's our relationship with others. Forgiving others is a choice we must make. Just like we won't *feel* like forgiving ourselves, we also won't *feel* like forgiving others. We may not be able to forget, but we can choose not to dwell on the hurt. We can choose to put it in God's hands so we can heal and move forward in our relationships.

Learning forgiveness is essential for walking alongside your young adult kids because some of their choices will hurt your heart. It's essential for being a mother-in-law because the people your kids choose to marry are also imperfect. It's needed for being an active grandparent because as your grandkids get older it may feel like they need you less or choose to do fewer things with you. If you choose to mentor others in this season of life, forgiveness will help you wipe the slate clean and keep your heart available for God to use however He sees fit. When hurt happens, we can lash out, sulk quietly, or forgive. Forgiveness is the best choice.

Courage

The enemy is the accuser and often kicks into gear as our kids get closer to leaving. He works hard to steal our joy. You and I have to have the courage to own what's ours and let our kids own what's theirs. Why is it that we moms tend to own more than what is ours? Why do we blame ourselves for our kids' sin issues? In parenting, our imperfect bumps up against our kids' imperfect and then we take the blame for all of it!

Sure, our guidance or lack of guidance can affect outcomes in our children's lives to some extent. This is why we tried our best to parent intentionally. Yes, there were times we were too tired or too overwhelmed to get it right, but the truth is we did the best we could with the knowledge and capacity we had. We laid the foundation, now they have to build their house as they launch into adulthood. They are responsible for their own decisions going forward, and they were also responsible for many of their decisions growing up.

We'll talk about this more later, but we also have to have the courage to not enable our now-adult kids. This is another reason why we have to let go of guilt. We can't feel "obligated" to make up for our shortfalls. We have to let our young adult kids feel the consequences of their choices. Resist bailing them out. Require them to pay rent if they're still living at home. Send them packing if they refuse to abide by the house rules. It's courage that helps us to do that as well.

Turn Guilt into Gratitude

As we apply the antidotes to the Perfection Infection—humility, confidence, grace, forgiveness, and courage—we slowly turn the tide of guilt to gratitude. With humility, we understand that not one of us is perfect and that God doesn't expect us to be perfect on this side of heaven. With confidence, we move from the guilt of "I can't" to the gratitude of "God can." With grace, we're grateful that God's gift washes over misplaced guilt. With forgiveness, we find freedom from the chains of guilt. Finally, we use courage to untangle ourselves from feeling responsible for things that aren't ours to own. We also stand firm on helping our young adults grow and take responsibility for the things that are theirs. As we transition into the encore season of life, we have to let the Perfection Infection go. This allows us to replace guilt with gratitude for the eighteen or more years we've had to lead, love, and enjoy this child.

Truth for Today:

"There is now no condemnation
for those who are in Christ Jesus."

Romans 8:1

Take the Next Step:

When you're tempted to compare yourself to
another mom on social media, at church, at the
store, at work, or in your neighborhood, say to yourself,
"She has a backstory I don't know." That will pull
you back from the ledge of comparison and plant
you on the firm foundation of reality.

Talk with God:

*Lord, sometimes guilt weighs me down. I know that's not
how You desire for me to live. Help me stop comparing and
leave condemnation behind. Show me how to turn guilt into
grace and gratitude. Thank You for the years I've had to lead,
love, and enjoy this child. Thank You for the coming years I
have to continue to love, encourage, and enjoy them as they
walk into their adult years. In Jesus' name, amen.*

Chapter 3

LET GO OF OPINIONS

It was shortly after our oldest daughter's wedding when someone asked me how it was being a mother-in-law. I told them that with adult children I've learned you now belong to the "keep it shut" club. "It seems you do a lot of *hmm* and *aah* responses when you hear about decisions they're making," I added.

It's true. Your kids are now living their own lives, making their own choices, and their decisions may not be something you like or agree with. Because of this, one of the most important things we need to let go of is our opinions.

Opinions and Expectations

If we expect a kid to be a mini-me we'll be sorely disappointed. They have their own style, their own likes and dislikes, and their own ideas. As our kids launch into their own lives it becomes easy to want to play the "I didn't raise you this way" card.

Certainly there is a time to remind them of their heritage or upbringing, but that card needs to be used sparingly . . . so it's more effective.

Don't like your son's beard? *Keep it shut.*

Don't care for your daughter's hair color? *Keep it shut.*

Don't agree with your child's parenting style? As long as your grandkids aren't in danger, you'll have to learn to be quiet. *Keep it shut.*

Don't like the job he or she has? *Keep it shut.*

Don't like how they're handling their money? *Keep it shut.* And don't rush to bail them out . . . let them feel the consequences when they've made poor choices, lest the same mistakes recur.

Of course, if your young adult is still depending on you in some way, you do have a vote in their life. However, you need to reserve that vote for things that really matter . . . and hair color doesn't really matter. Yes, even blue. And yes, even for your family pictures.

I speak from experience on this one. Our middle child, Erica, is our artist. "Free spirit" would be a good way to describe her, as well. Her hair has been pink, blue, silver, red, and many shades in between. It was my friend Brenda Garrison who challenged me about this issue in her book *Love No Matter What.* Brenda said, "If I make purple hair an issue, I become background noise in their lives. I didn't come this far as a mom to become background noise."[2]

This is why we need to resist sharing our opinions with our

kids. We want our voice to matter. To make a difference in their life. We don't want them to tune us out, so we need to use our words well. In fact, we need to offer far more affirmation than anything else. If they ask for our opinion, then yes, share it (kindly and carefully)! If they don't, pray for the change you'd like to see and keep it shut. This is very hard for most of us so let's dig into this a little bit more.

The Power of Affirmation

I sat across the table from a woman who was shedding tears over her recent interaction with her mom. Through her tears she said, "Just once. Just once I'd like to hear my mom say, 'great job.' Instead, all I get is how my brother would have handled the situation better or how I should have done something differently." This woman's mother desperately needs to learn to keep it shut. Even more, she needs to understand the power of affirmation.

You and I can be too negative. We can be too critical. But we can rarely be too positive. We can rarely provide more affirmation than what our loved ones need. As parents, we want our kids to be all they can be and too often we think the way to do that is to point out their deficits—the places they need to grow. The truth is, our affirmations will produce better results in their life and do far more to help them make the changes they need to make. Affirmations are best when they are specific. The more specific they are the more genuine they feel to the recipient.

Rather than telling them they're "good," tell them *what is good*—their accuracy, focus, efficiency, kindness, or honesty. Use the words "because" or "and" with a second more specific sentence to provide proof.

Calling out who they are is a powerful gift:

> "You're a man of integrity and I love how you handled that situation with your daughter."
> "You showed wisdom and tact because that problem with your coworker was tricky."
> "You are such an incredible artist and I'm amazed at the beautiful things you create."
> "You are so thoughtful. Thank you for paying attention to the details of my life and giving me such a meaningful gift."

We're never too old to need affirmation from our parents. My friend in tears is in her midfifties. If her mother began to replace the snide comments, hints, and critical words with encouragement and affirmation, it would change my friend from the inside out. Not only that, it would transform their mother-daughter relationship even this late in the game!

Pray, Don't Say

In Galatians 5 we're introduced to something called the fruits of the Spirit. These are things we experience when we spend time with God and He's in the driver's seat of our life. Think of an apple tree that, when given water, sun, and fertilizer, produces beautiful, yummy fruit. That's us. When we drink in God's truth and let Jesus lead us, we too produce fruit. Galatians 5:22–23 (ESV) tell us we experience "love, joy, peace, patience, kindness, goodness, faithfulness, gentleness, self-control." The fruits we particularly need as we fight the temptation to share our opinions when they're not requested are love, patience, kindness, gentleness, and self-control.

When we're trying to stop doing something, stopping isn't usually enough action to find success. Stopping something *and* starting something in its place, however, usually assures victory. This is why in those moments when we're tempted to say something we probably ought not say, we need to pray instead. Think: *Pray, don't say.*

God is far more powerful than you or me. He has the ability to change our kids from the inside out. Of course, His timing is not our timing and His ways are not our ways. That's where we need patience. We have to trust that He loves us and our kids more than we can imagine and ever understand. That's why He sent His Son to this earth to die on a cross for us. That's also why we need to pray—often in place of and most definitely before—saying anything.

If you're married and both of you are believers and you haven't prayed together as a couple much, the empty nest season is a perfect time to get started! Prayer *is* your work as a parent in this season. Your influence in prayer is much stronger than your influence in words. Now that it's usually just Mark and me in the car when we drive somewhere, that's become one of our favorite times to pray. One of us will say, "Let's pray for the kids," and we'll just "popcorn prayer" (each of us praying a sentence or two alternating back and forth like popping popcorn) until we've prayed for each of our kids and grandkids.

Anytime we pray, we're releasing our worry and stress and handing it over to God. He can do way more than we can. He'll also give us the clarity and then strength to let go of what we need to while also giving us the vision for what's ahead in this new season of life!

Let Go of Authority

You've spent twenty years being the authority in your child's life and that's why you're so accustomed to offering your thoughts, direction, and opinions. Once your kids are on their own, however, you've now passed the baton of authority. They are now under the authority of God and certain human authorities: work supervisors, laws of the land, and so forth. This is so hard and it's even harder when they become parents themselves. Remember that when your kids have kids, their authority with their kids trumps yours. Let's talk about that for a few minutes.

It was the Sunday after my third grandchild was born in Texas when a neighbor asked me if I was heading south that week. I told her I wished that I was, but Erica and Kendall had asked me to wait to come until Marie, who was born eight weeks early, was home. "Well, did you tell them that it's grandma's prerogative to come now if she wants?" she responded. I smiled and said that I wanted to respect Erica and Kendall's wishes.

The conversation bothered me, but I wasn't sure why. However, it was several other conversations with both of my girls that helped me formulate my thoughts. The girls shared with me disappointing stories friends have shared of dealing with moms or mothers-in-law after a baby is born, such as:

- One young mom's mother insisted on coming the week that the baby was born. This grandma pulled no punches in saying that she was there to hold the baby and nothing else. She said she'd hold the baby so her daughter could keep up with meals and laundry. *So selfish.*
- Another young mom's extended family—all eight of them—came to visit for a week arriving the day everyone came home from the hospital. They didn't stay at a hotel . . . they stayed in the small home of this young couple. *So inconsiderate.*
- Another friend of one of my daughters shared that when they visit her in-laws or when the in-laws come to town to visit or take care of the kids, Grandma and Grandpa don't follow the instructions for bedtimes or boundaries that Mom and Dad have set for their kids. The grandparents communicate that they get so little time with the grandkids that they "deserve" to have the extra time with the kids, plus the kids didn't seem tired anyway.

They also have let it be known (by their attitudes and actions) that they believe Mom and Dad's guidelines, boundaries, and routines are foolish. *So disrespectful.*

- Another young mom said that when her in-laws come and visit, it's not giving her a break, it's adding to her usual chores. They rarely offer help and they insist on eating out rather than home-prepared meals. This young mom finds eating out unenjoyable with little ones, not to mention the fact that eating out doesn't fit this young family's budget. *So stressful.*

- Yet another mom shared her frustration about a grandparent who smokes and has cats. This mom doesn't want her kids around smoke, and two of her kids have animal allergies. This grandma complains that her daughter-in-law is keeping her from her grandkids, which isn't true. The daughter-in-law graciously offers to meet Grandma at a park or invites her to their home (smoking not allowed), but instead of being grateful for the offer, Grandma digs in and refuses to see the kids unless it's on her terms. *So stubborn.*

There are no "grandma's prerogatives." There are only Mom and Dad's prerogatives. A grandparent's job is to help and encourage, offering assistance within the lifestyle and routines of this new family.

I am blessed to have had my parents model this transfer of authority to me. As grandparents, they have given much love, been available, but never once pulled the "grandparent prerogative" card. Anytime I left my kids in their care, I never worried if they would follow my instructions. When they visited, they offered to help with meals, dishes, laundry, running kids to activities, or whatever was going on that day. When they've come to town for weddings and our house is filled with adult kids and their families, they have offered to stay in a hotel for the night.

When your kids have kids, check your expectations and remember that your job is to defer to Mom and Dad's wishes—*even if you don't agree with them*. Be a good house guest if you have to travel to visit family. Build trust by doing what your child and their spouse ask you to do.

When (and if) grandkids come along, the goal is to have a good relationship between Mom and Dad and Grandma and Grandpa. Understanding the transfer of authority and that "grandparent prerogative" doesn't exist is a start to making that relationship strong!

What about Matters of the Faith?

"Jill, I understand the 'keep it shut' principle, but what about things of the faith? Even eternity? Shouldn't we share truth?" The answer to that is a hearty yes. It's the "how to share" where we have to broaden our perspective.

Some of your kids may not be walking with the Lord. To watch them leave behind the foundation of faith you gave them growing up breaks your heart. To watch them struggle in life without the strength and wisdom of the Lord tears you apart. To see grandchildren being raised without a firm foundation of faith is so hard.

When it comes to truth, however, sometimes our actions speak louder than our words. One of the biggest reasons the younger generation struggles with faith, and specifically the church, is due to the hypocrisy they see. They believe the church is much more judgmental than loving. Sometimes that perception is accurate. At other times they confuse disagreement with a lack of love (in other words, "You don't love me if you don't agree with me"). We can do something about the first reason, but not so much about the second reason.

The late evangelist Billy Graham stated with wisdom, "It is the Holy Spirit's job to convict, God's job to judge, and my job to love." As parents, we could stand to tattoo that statement on our hearts. Jesus operated with the beautiful blend of truth and love. We read in Luke 19:1–10 how He went to the home of Zaccheus, a tax collector who was considered one of the worst kind of sinners. Just the act of stepping into Zaccheus's world and home was an act of love, and He shared truth while He was there. He lovingly interacted with the woman at the well while speaking truth to her (John 4:1–26). In both cases, Jesus' actions were as powerful as His words.

One of the most important actions of truth is letting our kids know that no matter what, they're a part of your family. No matter what, you love them. No matter what, they are accepted. It's important to understand that acceptance doesn't mean agreeing with. It means accepting the reality of their circumstances. You may not agree with them and their choices, but no matter what, they will always be a part of your family.

> **One of the most important actions of truth is letting our kids know that no matter what, they're a part of your family. No matter what, you love them.**

Where too many Christian families go wrong is believing they can't have a relationship with a grown child with whom they disagree or a child who is living a life outside of God's ways. When we look at the example of Jesus, however, we see that He put Himself right in the middle of the lives of those who were far away from Him. He didn't separate Himself from them; He pursued relationship with them (having a relationship is usually the prerequisite for then being able to speak truth), and He challenged those far from Him toward godly lives.

Sometimes our actions with our adult children speak far louder than our words. We have certainly found this to be true with our son Evan.

Evan fought same-sex attraction for many years. We initially discovered this when he was in junior high after we found he'd been in places online he should not have been. After meeting with a counselor for several months, the counselor told us he felt it was a short-lived bump in the road through adolescence. Evan later said, "The only problem was, it wasn't. I continued to secretly deal with it more through high school.

But I decided, somewhat subconsciously, out of protection for myself and my family, this was something that I just needed to package up and toss in the corner because there was no way I wanted to talk about it with anybody and no way that I was going to accept it. So I suppressed it. For a very long time."

Evan grew up, and everything seemed okay from the outside, but he told us later that, though he was pursuing a heterosexual lifestyle, "This was the life that I wanted so badly, but I couldn't help but be scared that it might not fix my inner conflict like I wanted it to. And there wasn't a soul in the world who knew of my dilemma. I struggled alone."

As his inner turmoil grew, his relational life began to unravel. One Sunday afternoon our phone rang. Recalling that day, Evan said, "I had reached a breaking point. The only people I knew I could trust were my parents. I called my dad and just began to weep. I was hurting. And I was exhausted. I was so tired of holding it in and I just wanted to explode. My mom got on the phone, too, and as I cried for what seemed like hours, I told my parents everything. They listened and cried with me. This was just the beginning of very hard conversations and no more secrets."

As his mom, hearing the anguish in my son's soul broke my heart. He told us things we had not known, things he had bottled up and was now coming to us with. It was a heart-wrenching conversation, to say the least.

I wanted to share some of Evan's journey because I want you to understand the layers of struggle in his story. Whatever it is that our kids struggle with—sexuality, eating disorders, addiction, insecurity, perfectionism, depression, anxiety, and the list goes on—there are no easy answers. There are no quick fixes. As we navigate these difficult parts of our kids' lives, we need to be bridge-builders not just gatekeepers. The Sunday afternoon Evan called us was one of the most painful parenting moments I can remember. We were on the phone with him for several hours, tears flowing nonstop from all three of us. He was in such a place of deep despair and I hated that we were too far away to show up on his doorstep. I wanted to hold him and just let him cry.

When our kids struggle, we have to remember there's a depth of pain we often don't see. But it's there. They may even act like things are okay, but deep down it's likely there's a tug-of-war going on in their heart. The human experience has so many emotional layers to it.

> This was no longer a social issue we were just aware of. Now it was very personal and a human heart that we love was in the middle of it.

There's often a tug-of-war going on in our heart, too. As I processed what Evan shared in the following days, weeks, and now years, I've been conflicted internally as a Christian and as a mother. This wasn't something I ever anticipated I'd have to walk through. This was also no longer a social issue we were just aware of. Now it was very personal and a human heart that we love was in the middle of it.

This is why we need to lead with love and grace. Respond,

not react. Relationship over just being right. Compassion over compliance. Love over lectures. It's important to believe there is right and wrong, but our job is the same either way: our job is to love well.

Sometimes love is speaking truth; however, if you've not built a relational bridge to deliver that truth in a relational way, your words are wasted. Are you safe to talk to? Are you a good listener? Do you ask questions in place of lecturing?

We have tried to walk out our relationship with a balance of love, truth, and grace. Galatians 5:6 tells us, "The only thing that counts is faith expressing itself through love." So love is more important than anything. As Billy Graham reminded us, that's our job. The Bible mentions love at least 310 times. That's a lot of instruction on what we're supposed to do. When Jesus was asked what the most important commandments were, He said we were to love God and love people (see Mark 12:28–31).

Evan knows we love him no matter what. He's ours. He belongs. We love him unconditionally—even if we don't agree with every decision he makes. Loving him well has opened doors to show love to others whose families have alienated or disowned them and has challenged us to continually evaluate how much better we can love on people than we did before.

When we don't agree with our kids, we can still accept them. We may sit in different places on an issue, but they can still know they are loved and that they belong. Certainly truth can be shared and talked about but it's not the bulk of the conversations. Our actions speak truth as well. Same for kids who are in a spiritual desert. We ask God for wisdom in just about every conversation we have with them. What do You want me to say, Lord? What do You want me to not say? How do I need to respond to be Your hands and feet? Where do I need to affirm her? What opinions do I need to keep to myself so I'm not in the way of what You're doing in his life?

If you have kids who are not walking with the Lord, ask God to help you stay away from unnecessary opinions. Ask Him to show you when to share truth and when to live truth. My experience is that you'll live out truth much more than you'll speak about truth. That's following in Jesus' footsteps.

What about at my house?

Yes! At your house, you can call the shots . . . to some degree. Why to some degree? Because we still have to be careful about throwing around opinions that simply do not matter and might communicate criticism even if you don't intend for it to.

However, at your house you can set your own boundaries or guidelines that you feel are important. Got a child who smokes? You might choose to let them know that at your house they can't smoke or they need to smoke outside. Taking care of the grandkids? It's okay to have Nana and Papaw rules at Nana and Papaw's house, as long as they don't usurp Mom and Dad's rules. Do you have a young adult child still living with you? As long as you are still supporting them in some way (living at home is supporting them), it's okay to have agreements about rent paid (and yes, any young adult child who is not in college but is still living with you should be contributing to the cost of the abode they live in), cellphone paid (if they're still on your plan), and basic life expectations set (you can live here if you have a job and keep a job). We'll talk about this more in the next chapter, but anything less than this falls into the enabling category, and enabling our young adult kids is not loving them well.

What about adult kids who are living together or who are in a same-sex relationship? What about when they come for a visit? Do they stay in the same room at your home? For all these situations and more, you must come to decisions that honor the Lord, work for your family situation, and ensure your adult child feels respected.

No Comment Necessary

I love what Louie Giglio says about opinions: "Maturing is realizing how many things don't require your comment." By the time we hit the empty nest, most of us are beginning to understand this to some degree. As our kids launch, however, we easily fall back into sharing opinions in an effort to push our kids in the right direction and sometimes in a misguided effort to simply maintain connection. Don't do it. For the sake of relationships, let go of sharing your unrequested opinions today.

Truth for Today:

"The Holy Spirit produces this kind of fruit in our lives: love, joy, peace, patience, kindness, goodness, faithfulness, gentleness, and self-control."

Galatians 5:22–23a (NLT)

Take the Next Step:

In your marriage, as a parent, with a friend, at church, or in the workplace there are so many occasions in the past when you likely would have commented. Start paying attention to the opportunities you have to withhold comment. Practice *pray, don't say* every time you have a chance.

Talk with God:

Lord, it's Your job to convict, it's Your job to judge, and it's Your job and my job to love. I confess that sometimes I try to take over Your jobs. Show me how to love well. Teach me how to live truth. Help me keep my mouth shut when situations simply don't need my comment. In Jesus' name, amen.

Chapter 4

LET GO OF TRADITIONS

Several years ago, we didn't spend Thanksgiving with a single one of our five children. Did it feel odd? Yes. Was it the best for everyone? We think so.

Our oldest daughter and her husband alternate holidays with his family and our family; that year Thanksgiving was with his family. Our oldest son was living in California and coming home for Thanksgiving just wasn't in his budget. Our middle daughter, her husband, and our granddaughter were already expected at two different Thanksgiving gatherings on his side of the family. Our second youngest spent the holiday with some friends, and our youngest and his then-fiancée would have been happy to join us, but we decided to give them the freedom of no expectations and the ability to enjoy the day fully with her family. Instead of gathering our immediate family, Mark and I drove a couple hours to spend time with our parents, who we rarely see on holidays.

I love the holidays but I don't love them more than my family. I love traditions but I don't love them more than the people I share those traditions with. Too often the biggest "gift" given to family is guilt. Sometimes the most loving thing we can do is give our family freedom. That's why, to some extent, it's important to let go of traditions in the empty nest season of life.

The Value of Traditions

Traditions have their place in our families because they're part priority and part identity. Traditions tether us to the things that are valuable to us. They connect us to the past. Often passed on from one generation to the next, traditions are stories, beliefs, rituals, customs, and activities that help foster a sense of belonging and may even pass along family values.

The priority part of traditions helps us maintain a commitment to the important things that draw our family together. Because family members don't want to miss out, traditions often motivate us to gather. It was our son Evan, now living in Australia, who introduced me to the concept of FOMO: Fear Of Missing Out. One Christmas when he was too far away to come home, he said he was experiencing serious FOMO. He missed gathering with family, eating persimmon pudding (one of our family traditions), and playing endless games of euchre (also one of our family rituals).

The identity part of traditions helps connect us to the values that form the foundation of our family. Traditions like serving at a homeless shelter once a month or attending church together on Christmas Eve connect us to purpose and identity. They carry out the values that mean something to our family.

So if traditions are so important, why in the world am I suggesting that empty nest mamas have to let go of them? The key is the little phrase I used above: "to some extent." Let's dig into that a little bit more.

Traditions are a valuable part of family life. However, we need to learn to separate the difference between the "what" and the "when." The "what" are the activities, rituals, and customs we all enjoy. If these are missing, birthdays don't feel like birthdays or Christmas doesn't feel like Christmas. The "when" is the time we'll prioritize to gather or participate in the "what." The changes that have to happen during the empty nest season of life include both the what and the when. Let's explore both and what might need to change.

The "what"

The traditions that connect us to our family's habits give meaning to certain times of the day or the year. It could be daily habits like what happens at breakfast every morning or dinner every night, and it could be holiday or celebration related. These are the things that become important to our family members.

Sometimes habits fade naturally. When our kids were growing up, our family celebrated birthdays with birthday breakfast.

We had cake and ice cream for breakfast when one of the kids or Mark or I had a birthday. With seven of us in the family, we had birthday breakfast almost monthly for some parts of the year! The kids loved that tradition.

Anne's first birthday away from home was her freshman year of college. She said the day felt like something was missing without birthday breakfast! However, as each birdie flew away, birthday breakfast dwindled. The last birthday breakfast I coordinated was our youngest, Austin's, birthday, which happened to fall on his first day of classes his freshman year of college at Moody Bible Institute. With the help of a friend who worked on campus, I made sure he had cake and ice cream in the morning. He was so surprised, and it meant the world to have that connection to home his first time away.

Anne has carried the tradition forward into her family, but for the rest of us birthday breakfast has faded away. It served its purpose during our child-rearing years. It celebrated each individual and inserted fun into our family environment. We still celebrate the individual on their birthday, but just in different ways now that we're spread farther apart. The heart is still the same; how we carry it out is different.

Holiday traditions may center around food or activities. Our family's Christmas wouldn't be complete without persimmon pudding or Beef House rolls. The persimmon pudding tradition started with my grandmother, and my sisters and I still carry it on. Our kids love persimmon pudding too. This past Christmas Anne watched me make the hundred-year-old recipe, mentioning that someone in the next generation needed to carry on the tradition. The Beef House rolls started with our own family. Christmas and Thanksgiving are the only time of the year we allow ourselves those supersized yeast rolls that are so yummy!

Sometimes, however, the "what" needs to be evaluated. In fact, one of the best things you can do as an empty-nester is to do a holiday tradition audit with your family. You might just send a text to family members and ask, "As we're heading into Christmas, what food is a must-have for you?" You can do the same for holiday activities. When my friend Karen did a holiday audit, she found that half the traditions she stressed over making happen weren't even important to her family. She simplified her holidays immensely when she asked a few intentional questions.

"Whats" can also change. Handling gift exchanges, how the holiday meal is managed, where the family gathers, and so on; these are likely to be adapted in some way in this new season of life. My friend Beth's family does a modified white elephant exchange. I'll let her explain:

Long ago we started doing a simple activity with just the adults in our family. All the kids go in another room to watch a Christmas movie, and we have our own gift exchange. Each adult brings three $5 gifts wrapped and tagged simply to a man or woman. They all go in a box, we draw numbers, and then select gifts in that order. We allow stealing as well. We get to laughing so hard the kids always want to peek and find out what's so funny. Every child who turns 18 gets to decide if they want one more year of getting gifts from us, or to join the adults. Every single 18-year-old has chosen to join the adults because it is big and loud and fun!

Other families I know are giving "experiences" instead of material gifts. These kinds of gifts can fit the budget, interest, and ages of the family. They also foster family togetherness! We're trying to figure out a way to simplify gift giving at Christmas now that our family is so much larger. I'm sure in another year or two we'll have figured out a new Savage family tradition that will serve us well for that season.

The "when"

Once you've decided what traditions are most meaningful to your family and still practical to do in this season of life, the "when" of traditions is probably the biggest change that may need to happen. There's nothing magical about the fourth Thursday in November that makes it Thanksgiving, other than it being considered a national holiday and the fact that most businesses are closed. You can celebrate Thanksgiving whenever it works for your family. In fact, last September our son Evan came home from Australia for my mom's eightieth birthday celebration. We decided to gather all our kids and their families the Thursday night before her birthday to have our family's Thanksgiving celebration . . . in September! We took advantage of Evan being home and made it happen. And yes, we had both persimmon pudding and Beef House rolls!

Sometimes gathering the family is affected by distance and sometimes it's affected by their other obligations. This is where we can give our kids the gift of holiday freedom. There's nothing worse than feeling like you're expected at two family holiday celebrations in one day. Add in a divorce or two and that could increase to three or four celebrations in a day.

> **Sometimes gathering the family is affected by distance and sometimes it's affected by their other obligations. This is where we can give our kids the gift of holiday freedom.**

Not to mention new traditions the new family wants to set themselves. Obligation isn't fun, and running from house to house trying to make everyone happy is hardly an enjoyable activity.

If you have a single adult child, he or she may feel obligated to spend the holidays with "the parents" as a duty. While they don't have the same pull between two families as married kids do, they very likely do have a life outside of family. Giving them the gift of freedom is also appropriate because you're recognizing the individual they are and the new life they are establishing themselves.

If you have a married child, you might suggest that they alternate holidays with the in-laws. If you have more than one child married, getting them to alternate the same holidays the same year can be even more helpful. Once all the kids are married, that may mean you only gather every other Thanksgiving or Christmas, but you'll find new traditions for the off years (a getaway for yourself somewhere pretty and warm?) and everyone will fully enjoy it when it's your turn to gather. This can be a huge stress-reliever for those who are feeling the tug-of-war between two places they'd like to be. One mom I know has been doing this for years with her siblings and has found it very helpful. As they're all starting to have grandkids, they're actually talking about getting extended family together only in the summer in an effort to allow their new immediate families to create their own traditions for the holidays. This is a beautiful gift they're considering. There's no guilt for when they won't be gathering for the holidays, but rather they're just enjoying when they are gathering in the summer.

Another option is to set a new tradition in place. For instance, maybe your family always celebrates Thanksgiving the Saturday after Thanksgiving instead of Thursday. Or maybe Christmas is always the Saturday before or after Christmas. These kinds of new traditions honor those who want to gather with both sides of their family but moves the tradition away from the actual holiday day. Letting go of expectations and offering flexibility, love, and freedom brings families closer together than pouting over not celebrating "like we used to."

Forging New Traditions

It all started four years ago with a rest area brochure my then eighty-year-old dad picked up about exploring the Underground

Railroad in southern Indiana. I asked him why the brochure interested him and he said he thought it would be fun to do. I asked him when he was going to do it and he said, "Well . . . probably never, if I'm honest." I said, "Then let's do it! You and Mom and Mark and I. Let's make it happen." We set a date for our trip, made it happen, and had a blast.

At the end of that trip, I asked, "Where do you want to go next?" Mom said she'd always wanted to explore Galena, Illinois, so we did that the next summer. The third year it was Holland, Michigan, because Mom had also always wanted to go there. This past year Dad wanted to go to Franklin, Tennessee, to explore the Civil War sites, so we made it happen again.

We've now begun a new tradition of taking my parents on what we call their "bucket list trips" in our empty nest years. My parents won't be around forever—Mom's eighty and Dad's eighty-four. My two younger sisters are still raising families, so Mark and I are the ones who have the freedom to make these trips happen. We love this time we get to spend doing something fun together!

Another new tradition we've begun in the last year is Cousins' Weekend. Our oldest daughter has two children ages seven and nine. Our other daughter also has a seven-year-old. The cousins love playing together and of course, we love being with them. Last year we set aside one weekend a month—usually the second Saturday of the month—to host Cousins' Weekend. The grandkids arrive on Saturday afternoon and stay until Sunday afternoon. They so look forward to those weekends because they get to play with their cousins, they get to do fun activities—we usually try to do seasonal activities like carving pumpkins in October—and they get our full attention. Sometimes we plan something fun to do like a trip to the zoo, and sometimes we just let the kids play all weekend with a tea party thrown in for fun.

While Erica's family lived in town, for the first year of Cousins' Weekend Anne's family lived a little over an hour away, so we'd meet them halfway to connect and do the kid transfer. Our son-in-love recently changed jobs and they now live in town, making Cousins' Weekend a bit easier! We find that twenty-four hours is just the right amount of time, allowing the kids plenty of time to play, allowing us plenty of time to enjoy them, and then heading them back home before there are too many squabbles. It also gives their mom and dad one weekend a month to themselves.

My friend Julie has been hosting Grammy Camp for years. This is Cousins' Weekend on steroids! She often picks a theme (e.g., American history, mountains, water sports, space, a Bible verse) and they center their activities around that theme for one week in the summer. They do crafts, go to museums and festivals, and have fun together. She takes pictures throughout the week and then makes each family a Grammy Camp photo album for Christmas. She says she's trying to make family memories that will last beyond her.

The first year Austin went to college, Mark and I started taking a kickboxing class together at 7:00 every morning.

Something like that was never an option before because we didn't want to be gone in the mornings while the kids were still in high school. When Austin left for college, we looked at each other and said, "Wow . . . our mornings are now our own. What might we do together that wasn't possible before?" We enjoyed the classes for about two years, until I tore the meniscus in my knee and the rotator cuff in my shoulder. The resulting surgeries ended my kickboxing career and our morning routine, but it was fun while it lasted!

We recently started gathering once a month with our kids and grandkids who are within driving distance for Mexican Food Monday. Everybody brings some Mexican food to share on the first Monday night of the month. We like being together as a family in this lighthearted, regularly scheduled monthly gathering. It's a great time to catch up on each other's lives, let the grandkids play, and sometimes enjoy a game together.

What new traditions might you forge in your newfound freedom? Maybe a girls' trip with your daughters and daughters-in-love? Maybe it's a family vacation at a cabin in the summer or a gathering somewhere every five years. Maybe it's making your "bucket list" happen as a couple if you're married, or with friends if you're not. If you're married, maybe it's doing something special as a couple each month or starting or joining a small group. It might be vacationing with family or friends on a regular basis or hosting a card club. Or, if you have grandkids, it could be creating your own Cousins' Weekend or Grammy Camp. The encore possibilities are endless!

Navigating Change

One of the hardest things to do as a parent is to allow change to happen as your kids get older. Their sphere of relationships grows exponentially when they have other important people in their lives, or if they marry and start a new family. These days I'm using phrases like these more often:

"We understand. It's not the day that's important. We'll find another time that works better!"

"Your heart is most important to us. We don't want to add any additional pressure by piling on expectations. If you can join us, we'll be thrilled, and if you can't, we understand."

"I love you. I love you the same no matter what decision you need to make for your sanity and what's best for your schedule."

My friend Addie said, "Sometimes we have to put into practice what is best for our family before our heart is fully on board. I was able to encourage them to do what was best for them and their families, but my heart still hurt at first. I had to pray a lot and trust that God would give me peace about our new normal!" That's such a good reminder for us. It's not easy to navigate these changes, but it's important.

Want to give your adult kids a beautiful gift? Give the gift of freedom. Flexibility. No expectations. Unconditional love. They will be ever so grateful.

Truth for Today:

"For everything there is a season,
and a time for every matter under heaven."

Ecclesiastes 3:1 (ESV)

Take the Next Step:

Do a holiday and/or birthday audit. Ask your family
members what means the most to them on the major
holidays or on their birthday. Then, with this new
information, adjust what you do moving forward.

Talk with God:

*Lord, I confess that change is hard! I like things to be
the way they've always been. Help me see that the only
sure thing that never changes is You. You are the same
yesterday, today, and tomorrow. Help me let go of the "when"
of traditions and to do what is best for our changing, growing
family. I don't want to "gift" my family guilt. Help me free
them of obligation and have a grateful heart for when we're
able to be together—even if it doesn't match the date
of the holiday on the calendar. In Jesus' name, amen.*

Chapter 5

LET GO OF YOUR CHILD'S PROBLEMS

It was a plan I thought was genius. A mom and dad I know allowed their daughter to move back home after she finished her college degree. They had two furnished, empty bedrooms on the main level but decided they didn't want to make things too comfortable for their little birdie who needed to fly, so they offered her a corner of their basement complete with classy tarp walls, a simple bed, dresser, and side table. Nothing fancy, but it provided her a roof over her head as she worked out the details of launching. Thanks to Mom and Dad's ingenuity, she was motivated to fly sooner rather than later.

Thirty years ago, when young adults launched, they flew out of the nest and rarely returned home. In 2015, due to school loan debt, cost of living, and weak job prospects, nearly half of twenty-five-year-olds were living with their parents. This was up from just 25 percent who were living with their parents in 1999![3]

Obviously, this reality has implications for the empty nest season of life. We have to learn how to help but not enable. We also need to become adept at transitioning responsibility to our young adults even if they're living at home for a time.

Then, of course, there are some kids who have a more difficult time launching into adulthood. These kids often struggle with mental health issues, addictions, and life-controlling problems. Not enabling is even more important for these kiddos. This is also when, more than ever, we have to let go of our children's problems.

Help in the Messy Middle

Once kids finish high school, they're legally considered adults. You and I both know that emotionally, logically, and educationally they still have a long way to go. Fellow author and speaker Susan Seay told me, "There is a difference between 'adult age' and 'being grown.' 'Adult age' is a legal term. 'Being grown' happens when they're willing to take personal responsibility for their decisions—both the good ones and the not-so-good ones." If they're still depending on you for anything, they're not yet grown. It's important for you to know that and for them to know that as well!

There's no one right way to launch kids, because they're all different and they all have different needs. Each of our five kids left home in a different way than their siblings. Number one went to two years of college, had the opportunity to live abroad and serve as a nanny for a semester, then got engaged (on the Eiffel Tower!) and married. Number two went to two years of college, then married and entered the workforce. Number three was married right out of high school and then earned her associate degree. Number four went to work after high school . . . no college. And number five is our only one who so far has finished his bachelor's degree. He got a job right before graduation and got married just a few weeks later.

With kids leaving in different ways and at different times, it's helpful to have some wise guidelines that both help us and help our kids in the messy middle. Let's explore some of these:

Let kids carry some of the weight of their privileges. Having a phone and driving a car are privileges that cost something. At some point we need to have them start paying a portion of those expenses. We had our kids pay 25 percent of their phone and car insurance from the time they turned sixteen or got their first job. This introduced them to the cost of the privileges they enjoy. Once they finished college or started working full-time, they eventually took over those expenses completely (sometimes there was a gradual responsibility over a few months, 25 percent to 50 percent to 75 percent to 100 percent to help them adjust to the cost).

If they are working and living at home, require some form of "rent" from them. They're using electricity, eating food, and enjoying a roof over their head. You don't have to charge them market value, just something that helps them develop the habit of paying bills and thinking about the cost of living in general. Beth and her husband told their kids who were in the messy middle of launching, "If you're working and in school you pay

$100 a month. If you are not doing one of those things, you pay $200 a month. And if you're not doing either, $300 a month." Their daughter was quick to complain that it didn't make sense to pay more if she was unemployed. Her parents suggested she might want to get a job then!

If they're living with you while job hunting, give them an expected time frame for what happens with work. They may be looking for their first "perfect" job, but if it takes longer than a month or two to find, make sure they understand you expect them to be working at a less-than-ideal job in the meantime (fast food, retail, whatever-will-pay-the-bills). To some degree this generation struggles with entitlement more than any generation before. They don't want to flip burgers to put food on the table. Don't be afraid to tackle their entitlement with this reminder that sometimes you have to do things you don't want to do until the right opportunity opens up to do what you do want to do.

Require a share of chores. Some of these can even offset rent. When our daughter Erica and her family lived with us for a while in her husband's transition out of the army, one of the "rent" agreements was that they managed the yard work. We spelled out how often we expected the grass to be mowed and what all we needed to be done. We live on two and a half acres, so this was an extensive job every week. Taking that responsibility off our plate was a huge blessing for us, better than rent money, especially in the summer!

Put everything in writing. This helps clarify expectations and gives you something to refer to when agreements aren't being kept. If they're living with you, make sure that you state in the agreement that if they don't hold up their side of the deal, you'll give them one warning only. If they don't carry their responsibility after that, you'll give them thirty days to find a new place to live. If it's the phone or car insurance they're not paying, make sure the written agreement is clear that you will turn off their phone or revoke their driving privileges if the payment isn't made within ten days of the day of the month it's due. This may sound harsh, but it's the way the real world works. If you don't pay your rent, you're evicted. If you don't pay your phone bill, your phone is turned off.

Stand by your agreements. We had one who ended up at the homeless shelter due to his not taking responsibility for his life. He also had his phone turned off and his car insurance cancelled, among a plethora of other consequences. We offered to take him to the shelter, but he chose to walk. It broke my heart, but it was absolutely the right thing to do for him and for us.

If you've had young adult kids living at home for a while and haven't required some of these things, you may want to have a "business meeting" with them. Explain that you're realizing that you haven't been helping them prepare for the real world as well as you need to. Then explain any changes you'll be making. Make sure you give them a thirty-day notice if you expect them to begin picking up expenses they haven't been responsible for. You've likely been thinking about this for a while, but it may be a complete surprise to them. They need time to budget for them and adjust to their new expenses. If you have a kid who needs help with budgeting, you might introduce them to Dave Ramsey's Financial Peace course—in fact, you could take the course with them to foster conversation and reinforce the principles. I also have a resource over in my online shop (www.JillSavage.org/shop) that helps parents and teens or young adults manage their money. It's called the *Financial Notebook for Parents and Teens*.

When Your Child Says "My Life, My Choice"

Parenting can be a messy process. Chuck Colson says, "Life isn't like a book. Life isn't logical or sensible or orderly. Life is a mess most of the time, and theology must be lived in the midst of that mess." Mark and I have certainly found that to be true.

Our young adult kids are making choices every day. Some of them are good choices and for those we are grateful (and we need to celebrate and encourage our kids when they happen)! Others may not be, and we need to be wise enough to understand different kinds of choices. For example, they may choose a hair or clothing style that you're not wild about. They may even sport a tattoo or two! Your child may join a club or choose a sport that you're not thrilled over. These are preferences, so don't sweat it.

As we've said, the brain isn't fully developed until age twenty-six, so some poor choices will occur due to immaturity or just foolishness. Proverbs 22:15 reminds us, "Folly is bound up in the heart of a child." Your child might handle money poorly, move out of the house without being ready, not take college seriously or drop out, even quit a job without a good reason or without another one lined up.

And then there are choices our kids might make that have more serious consequences: immoral behavior, rejecting the faith, substance use/abuse. The good news is that we have prayer on our side and we know the Lord cares deeply for our children.

The other good news is that, though some poor choices are to be expected, the brain optimally grows in failure. This means the brain grows *best* in failure! So failure—poor choices—is a part of growing, learning, and maturing (as long as we don't protect our kids from the consequences of those failures).[4]

The real stuff we may experience

As hard as it is, if we carry too much responsibility for their issues and don't learn how to detach from their problems—and we all will struggle to some extent—we will experience some of these realities:

Time drain—Their issues and needs too easily consume our time until there's no time for self-care.

Emotional drain—We're not only carrying our own emotional weight but also our child's. Eventually it becomes too much and can bring on anxiety.

Guilt and shame—If we mistakenly own something that's not ours to own, or we believe our kids reflect poorly upon us, we'll experience guilt and shame.

Desperation—We'll do "anything" to make things better for our kids. This often leads us to make poor choices ourselves.

Embarrassment—We are ashamed of our kids' behavior and hope people don't find out.

Shock—Depending on the nature of the "poor choice," there might be shock as you process something that might have seemed unthinkable.

Shattered dream—You may experience a shattered dream for your child or of what you thought your family would look like.

Judgmental extended family—You may need to determine how much to share with extended family. You'll have to deal with their reactions and their simplified strategy suggestions (e.g., "Well, if you only . . .").

Stress on marriage—There may be stress on the marriage when you and your spouse disagree on how to handle a situation.

Stress on finances—There may be financial stress as you determine how much to help financially.

Stress on siblings—Some choices can affect the dynamics of the family as siblings come to grips or possibly get asked by their sibling to "help."

Holiday/family gathering stress—There could be additional stress at family gatherings depending on the dynamics of what's happening behind the scenes.

Isolation—When we're overwhelmed, we tend to isolate

and stay away from relationships that would usually fill us up.

Grief—This might be the loss of a dream for our child. If so, you may experience all the steps of grief including denial and isolation, anger, bargaining, depression, and finally acceptance (of your new normal).

Control—You want to "whip them into shape" and it becomes tempting to step into control, so they'll do what you want them to do. (*Psst* . . . this never works the way we think it will!)

On top of all of those realities, this is also when we question our parenting. Author and speaker Carol Kent and her husband, Gene, are weathering the unthinkable. Their son—their only child—is serving a life sentence without the possibility of parole for committing murder. I once heard Carol say, "When your only offspring commits a murder, you can't think of yourself as a good parent." Carol's books *When I Lay My Isaac Down* and *A New Kind of Normal* share their story and lessons God has taught them along the way of this very difficult journey.

It's during times like these that the enemy throws his lies around and we easily get sucked into feeling inadequate and filled with shame. We also feel so alone and even more guilty because these aren't exactly the issues people are talking about on Facebook, Instagram, or even Sunday morning at church (though we should be). More than ever this is when we need to understand Satan's Lies and God's Replies from the "Getting

Started" section in an effort to untangle ourselves from the enemy's lies and stand firm in the truth of who we are.

Your Life, Your Choice

In the same way that your child can say, "My life, my choice," so can you. It's your life and you also have some choices to make. Let's explore those.

Choose unconditional love

"Love one another as I have loved you." John 15:12 ESV

When things are hard, we need to learn to speak love in a way that does not encourage or embrace our kids' poor choices but allows us to still embrace our kids. It may require us to accept their reality while helping them understand we don't agree with them or the choices they make. For instance, to our son who has a plethora of mental health and legal issues, I've often said something like, "I love you and I believe there's a wise young man inside you. I'm believing that person can show up should this situation ever happen again." This calls out the person I believe is in there while still communicating the choice wasn't a good one.

We need to pattern our love after God's love. Our relationship with Him is secure. We are the beloved of God and we don't have to prove anything. Our child is our beloved child; they shouldn't have to prove anything to get our love—they may have to prove something to get our trust, but that's a different issue. One mom said, "Initially I felt I needed to tell them periodically how I felt about their behavior, but I have come to understand they know how we feel and what we believe. I don't need to say it anymore. I do, however, need to keep affirming I love them despite their choices."

It's important to also notice that more often than not, Jesus was about relationship. Staying in relationship is important because when our kids hit rock bottom, we want them to come to us. One mom offered this encouragement about loving a child with an addiction: "Never give up. Keep loving the person with the disease of addiction wherever they are on their journey, and don't save your love only for their successes."[5] Her words "don't save your love only for their successes" was very convicting for Mark and me. It's their journey, they are not defined by their disease, and they are worthy of love regardless of how successful they are in their recovery. But at the same time, we can't make it easy for them to continue their use.

Ask yourself: What does unconditional love look like in my situation? Is there something unresolved inside that's keeping me from loving? Unforgiveness? Shame and embarrassment? Misplaced blame?

Choose to not let this define you or your family

"See what great love the Father has lavished on us, that we should be called children of God! And that is what we are!" 1 John 3:1

You are not defined by your child's choices. Your value is from your Creator. Your God never changes—He's the same yesterday, today, and tomorrow. Your child's choices may change yesterday, today, tomorrow, and every moment in between.

People in your church, in your small group, in your neighborhood, and wherever may try to define you by your child's choices. That's the reality of the human condition and judgment. You have to *know* who defines you and *know* that He never changes.

I once heard Dr. Emerson Eggerichs say, "If I'm deriving my identity *from* my children rather than bringing my identity in Christ *to* my children, I'm putting a pressure on them to perform so that I'll be happy. Then I'll resent them if they don't perform or if they do perform I'm falsely feeling good about myself." Resist the urge to define yourself by your child's successes or failures. It's an unfair pressure to put on anyone.

Ask yourself: What am I basing my identity on—something that changes every day or Someone who never changes?

Choose to accept your child

"Accept one another, then, just as Christ accepted you." Romans 15:7

I've said it before, but I believe it bears repeating: accepting doesn't mean agreeing with. If you're dealing with a big issue with your child, accepting simply means acknowledging and recognizing the reality of your child's circumstances. It's being a safe person to be honest with—one who listens, shows compassion and empathy, and leads with love.

Every human being has a core need to belong. We want to know that people believe in us, approve of us, and accept us for who we are. We especially long for this from our parents. In the midst of the messiness of life, we need to make sure our children know they are still loved and accepted. We want them to know they belong to us *no matter what*.

> **Accepting doesn't mean agreeing with; it simply means acknowledging and recognizing the reality of your child's circumstances.**

Practically, accepting is about asking questions. It's about being a reflective listener. It's about caring enough to know them well. It's not about lecturing or telling them what to do. When we accept, we become safe for them to be honest with.

You need to know that acceptance itself is a process. It requires us to be nonjudgmental. You might ask, "Can you be nonjudgmental and still disagree?" Yes, you can. You'll have to listen well, reflect what they're saying, and work to have a respectful conversation even in disagreement. You can challenge them with questions like, "Have you thought about this? Have you thought about that?" but you need to do it respectfully and without lecturing. When they feel safe with you, they're much more likely to ask for your help when they need it. They're also less fearful of being told, "I told you so."

Ask yourself: If acceptance is a scale of 1 to 10 with 1 being not accepting and 10 being fully accepting, where am I on the scale? What do I need to work on? Listening? Asking questions? Not lecturing?

Choose community

"Now you are the body of Christ, and each one of you is a part of it."
1 Corinthians 12:27

There's a story in Luke 5:17–26 about a paralyzed man whose friends wanted to take him to Jesus. They found where He was, but the crowd was so large that they couldn't get into the house, let alone with the stretcher their friend was lying on. So they got creative and took him up on the roof, removed tiles, and lowered their pal down to Jesus, stretcher and all. This man needed his friends' support!

If you're walking through a tough situation, you need a support team: other empty nest moms with prodigal kids, Al-Anon, Alateen, Celebrate Recovery, Facebook groups for parents. Don't be afraid to share your story. After all, the story of any one of us is in some measure the story of all of us. You're not the only one struggling. Even if you share your story with someone who isn't struggling as a parent, God may use them to connect the dots to another mom who is also struggling and feeling isolated and alone.

Ask yourself: Am I comfortable asking for help from other people? Am I doing it? What might be most helpful right now: Professional advice? A shoulder to cry on? Help running errands or keeping the house or business in order? A weekend away? Financial support? Who can I ask to help me get what I need?

Choose gratitude

"Give thanks in all circumstances; for this is God's will for you in Christ Jesus." 1 Thessalonians 5:18

When our kid is saying "my life, my choice" one of the most important choices we can make is to be thankful for small things. Start seeing small progressive steps. In *When I Lay My Isaac Down*, Carol Kent shared a prayer she penned in her journal.

Lord, I've been complaining so much about everything that's wrong with the Department of Corrections that I totally forgot to thank You for the corrections officer who treated me with respect and kindness when she took me through the security procedure last week. Thank You for the other CO who brought in new coloring books and crayons for Chelsea and Hannah and for the other young children during our last visit. Thank You for the smile I got from the girlfriend of one of the inmates I met last month in the visitation line. Thank You that J.P. was allowed to order tennis shoes through "the system" that will enable him to enjoy his love of running and staying physically fit with much greater comfort.[6]

In the midst of a terrible situation, she found gratefulness helped keep her heart in a better place. She was grateful for kindness shown, smiles returned, and acts of generosity that would have been missed if she hadn't been intentional about choosing gratitude.

Ask yourself: In my situation right now, what is one small thing I can be grateful for? (Take a moment and thank God for that right now.)

Choose to lovingly detach

"A man reaps what he sows." Galatians 6:7

The phone call came in the middle of the night. No parent wants to hear the voice of a police officer on the other end of the line. Our son Nicolai had been transported to the hospital for an overdose. This would make his sixth suicide attempt in four years. To say we were devastated and worn out would be an understatement. We were also fearful and worried and baffled at how to help our child we adopted at the age of nine from Russia.

As our kids become adults, they may still need our help on occasion. The challenge is figuring out how to help but not rescue or enable. As hard as it is, when our kids have recurring problems, we really do have to learn to let go of their problems.

It was just a few days after that phone call from the police officer when I met up with Marilee for dinner. The pain of the last few days was fresh, and I poured out my heart to my friend. A good fifteen years older than me, I'd known Marilee only in her empty nest years. I didn't know her kids or know her when she and her husband were raising their kids. However, God knew what He was doing when He connected the dots for us to meet for dinner this particular evening.

Our dinner took place in Atlanta, where I had traveled for some business meetings. I was supposed to leave on Sunday to drive to Atlanta, but I had delayed the trip by a day due to Nicolai's unexpected hospitalization. As I shared what we were dealing with, I finally blurted out something Mark and I were feeling but had never put into words. I said, "We love him, Marilee, but he hijacks our life all the time!" Marilee listened carefully. She asked questions. Then she shared their story of raising a child with mental health issues. I had no idea. She sincerely understood what we were dealing with.

After we talked for nearly an hour, Marilee said something to me I will never forget. "Jill, I know this will sound harsh to you, but I need to share some wisdom. The next time Nicolai is hospitalized, you need to go to the hospital and tell him how much you love him. Pray for him while you're there. Tell him you believe in him and then fifteen minutes later you need to walk out the door and go back to your life."

What???? I could barely comprehend what Marilee was saying. This was our son. He needed help. How could we do something that seemed like such a cold response? However, the next few days of my trip, I looked back on the last four years. Processing this with Mark, we had to admit that our "help" hadn't really helped at all.

> **Lovingly detaching means that I let go of my child's problems and place them in God's hands.**

This was Day 1 of learning about a concept called "lovingly detaching." It's a term often used in the addiction world where family members are encouraged to remain attached to the person but detached from their problems. Detaching with love means caring enough for others to allow them to learn from their mistakes. It also means that I no longer allow my loved one's actions, words, or behavior to affect my mood, identity, security, or plans. Lovingly detaching means that I let go of my child's problems and place them in God's hands. This is what Marilee was talking about.

Simple, but not easy. We mamas are fixers in our kids' lives. We kiss boo-boos and make everything right. We solve problems. We nurture, love, and care for. Detaching goes against our natural tendencies.

I believe it's even harder for this current generation of empty nest moms to do this because many of us have thrown ourselves into parenting with such devotion that some of us have lost ourselves along the way. We've "hyper-parented," trying to manage all aspects of our kids' lives in order to ensure the best outcome. In recent years the term "helicopter parents" was coined to describe "a style of parents who are over focused on their children. . . . They typically take too much responsibility for their children's experiences and, specifically, their successes or failures,"[7] explains Carolyn Daitch, director of the Center for the Treatment of Anxiety Disorders near Detroit. Licensed psychologist Ann Dunnewold addresses "overparenting" and says, "It means being involved in a child's life in a way that is overcontrolling, overprotecting, and overperfecting, in a way that is in excess of responsible parenting."[8]

Letting go of our kids' problems is hard enough as it is. If we've overparented at all, letting go of our kids' problems will be even more complicated. Yet it's something we must learn to do in order to truly help our kids and, in some cases, maintain our sanity.

Let's clarify with some definitions. Helping is being there or doing something for someone that they cannot do for themselves. Enabling is doing something for somebody that they could or should be doing for themselves. While we're defining things, let's throw in that controlling is doing for someone what *you* want them to do.

Some of this is by trial and error. There are no textbook answers. Each kid is different, so you have to listen to the Holy Spirit. Usually with these kids, it's not about what they say, it's about what they do. Some of these kids have been lying and manipulating for years. You can't believe what they say, but you can watch for actions that indicate progress.

It's okay to tell your child, "We will no longer work harder at this than you are." It's also helpful to ask yourself if your help has yielded fruit and progress or if the negative cycle has just continued on. When Mark and I asked ourselves that question concerning Nicolai, we got our answer about whether we were helping or enabling. Enabling it was, and that became the day we began to turn things in a different direction. It was evident our help really wasn't helping our son after all.

Ask yourself: Is a negative behavior cycle continuing even with help? Am I contributing to that? Am I letting them live in our house or giving them money that contributes to their continuing the negative cycle? Where am I in the current situation? Am I helping or enabling?

Choose unshakable faith

"Now faith is confidence in what we hope for and assurance about what we do not see." Hebrews 11:1

When God seems the most absent, He is the most present. There's always hope. When our child says, "My life, my choice," we need to choose faith, believing there's something still good in that person's heart. We have to find our strength in God when things are hard.

There are too many grandparents raising grandkids these days. This is a whole different journey and, honestly, they need their own separate book. However, it's possible your child's choice may put you in a position to have to make some choices yourself. If your child has children but is emotionally or physically unable to care for those children, will you step in and give them the stability they need? Will you believe that, with God's help, you can do that?

If your prayers are a mess, that's fine! It's to be expected.

Just pour your heart out to God. Search His Word for truth that will buoy your faith. One of the early books we read after our son came out was *Out of a Far Country: A Gay Son's Journey to God. A Broken Mother's Search for Hope*[9] by Christopher and Angela Yuan. Angela is Christopher's mom. Angela wasn't a believer early on in Christopher's life, but she met Christ and began to understand the power of prayer. She turned a spare shower into her prayer closet and interceded for her son faithfully for many years. He was a drug user and a drug dealer, involved in homosexual relationships, and even eventually served a prison sentence. However, his life was transformed by Christ in prison. Prayer makes a difference!

We have to ask ourselves,"Will I give up on Him? Or will my choice be faith? Unshakable faith?" God invites us to experience the victory of choosing faith even when it seems to make no sense. Part of faith is hope: Hope that God will get you through. Hope that your child has the ability to change. Hope that believes Matthew 9:26: With God all things are things are possible.

Have you prayed a messy prayer, spilling out your guts to God? You don't have to walk this alone. God knows what it feels like to have a child who breaks your heart. He deals with that every day in His relationship with us.

Ask yourself: What do I really believe about God? What do I really believe about prayer? Is it time to focus on my own faith journey so I can know that even when it isn't well with my circumstances it can still be well with my soul? Do I need to create a prayer room or set aside a day to fast and pray for my kids? Do

I need to get into a Bible study?

Are You Seeing Clearly?

The email arrived in my inbox one Tuesday morning. This mom was asking for prayer concerning conflict she and her husband were experiencing over their twentysomething daughter, who was a single mom and was still living in their home with her own child. She was asking for prayer that her husband would see things differently and stop wanting their daughter to leave home.

I'm betting my response was not what she expected as I challenged her to not minimize her husband's expressed frustration and concern. I also reminded her that her daughter's problems were not her problems and that as long as she kept trying to "help" her daughter she was actually enabling her to stay dependent upon them. Maybe it was time to set up an exit strategy, or require their daughter to pay some rent. Maybe they needed to set some boundaries so she did not expect free babysitting when she was working. Steps like those would help ease their daughter into the adult world she needed to be moving toward.

As our birdies are getting ready to fly, we must help transfer responsibility from us to our kids. When our kids make their own decisions and experience negative consequences from those decisions, we must let them feel the weight of the cost of their choice. The worst thing we can do is clean up their mess. The most loving thing we can do for them and for us is to let go of their problems.

Truth for Today:

"Give thanks in all circumstances."

1 Thessalonians 5:18

Take the Next Step:

Decide which "choice" you need to make a priority.
Put its accompanying Bible verse in front of your eyes
(e.g., write it on your bathroom mirror with a wet erase
marker, write it on an index card or sticky note and put
it where you'll see it, make it your locked screen phone
wallpaper). Be intentional about making that choice
rather than defaulting to an old way of responding.

Talk with God:

*Lord, it's so hard to let go. I confess I'm sometimes
emotionally entangled in my kids' problems. Help me
untangle. When they make poor choices, help me not be
defined by those choices, but rather be defined by You and
only You. I know my child is still growing and learning. Help
me turn my worries into prayers. In Jesus' name, amen.*

Chapter 6

LET GO OF IDOLS

It was a Tuesday evening when the phone call came in. Our son Nicolai was living in Oklahoma. He'd moved out there after high school to get a fresh start living with my sister, who is single. He did well for about five months and then he began to emotionally spiral. In an effort to not enable, she finally had to tell him to leave. He refused to get help and chose to live in his car for about a month. He eventually found a job and kept it long enough to secure an apartment with his girlfriend.

His voice on the other end of the line was tentative. We knew something had happened because he just couldn't get the words out. Finally, we understood why he had called. His girlfriend was pregnant. "Of course, we're planning on keeping the baby," he said.

They couldn't pay for utilities, so they were living without heat and sometimes without electricity. They often ate less than three meals a day. This was no environment to bring a child into. After we hung up, I told Mark I'd be the first one to call the Department of Child and Family Services to get that baby out of their home.

Over the next few weeks, however, they began to talk about adoption. I never had to make that call because a relative stepped up and offered to adopt the baby. Nicolai and his girl-friend agreed. Even though this little one calls us Aunt Jill and Uncle Mark, she is both our grandchild and our niece—think about that for a few minutes!

The night Nicolai called to tell us about the baby, I became physically ill. My response was more than disappointment. It was more than sadness. Those emotions are to be expected when hearing news of that kind. My concern for this new little life was tangible. My anger at our son's disregard for the things we'd taught him growing up was understandable.

However, when I was finally able to look at it from a spiritual perspective, I had to admit there was something deeper going on inside me. I was mortified. Embarrassed, even. If I was honest, *I was afraid of what people would think*. When I was finally able to admit that, I knew the issue I was dealing with: I'd made my children's behavior an idol. I was using them to define myself. In order to have a healthy relationship with my kids, I had to let go of my idols.

The "gods" We Worship

There is a story in the Bible about a time when the Israelites, who had left slavery in Egypt, were being led by Moses to the promised land. God had done great, miraculous things for His people—parted the Red Sea, provided daily food called manna, led them with a pillar of fire by night and a pillar of cloud by day. And yet when Moses was away on Mount Sinai for forty days receiving the Ten Commandments, they now questioned God's provision and took things into their own hands. They were worried Moses wouldn't return and they reverted to their "god worship." They brought together all their gold, melted it down, and formed it into the shape of a calf. Then, incredibly, they worshiped the golden calf. (You can read the whole story in Exodus 32.)

The first of the Ten Commandments is, "You shall have no other gods before me" or "besides" me. That's "gods" with a lower case "g." A "god" is anything to which excessive attention, devotion, or reverence is given. When we worship something we give it our focus, as the Hebrews did with the golden calf, making it an idol.

We unintentionally end up with idols in our life. When we elevate something as more important than God, when we revere anything rather than revering, worshiping, and being devoted to God, we have made other things idols. We may "worship" the creation or material objects or even our family stability. We may be on social media and expend time and energy on the number of likes our post gets. We can each cite examples of modern-day idols and what may be tempting to replace devotion to God within our own lives.

We must guard against devotion to anything other than God, because any other pursuit will fall short of delivering what we deeply long for. For example, we long for the fruit of the Spirit found in Galatians 5:22–23: love, joy, peace, patience, kindness, goodness, faithfulness, gentleness, and self-control. The more we worship God and only God, the more we experience that fruit. The more we worship "gods," the less we have that fruit in our life. Instead, we experience angst, anxiety, sadness, impatience, anger, harshness, and little self-control.

> The empty nest season of life has a way of bringing idols to the surface.

The empty nest season of life has a way of bringing idols to the surface. This is because our world has been turned upside down, our purpose in life has changed, and what was our "normal" is no longer. With the busyness of everyday mother-hood slowing down and our emotions being topsy-turvy, our identity takes a hit and our idols reveal themselves. Let's dig in and take a look at some of the idols we have to let go of.

Worry

Worry is the worship of our circumstances. Bet you've never thought of it that way. Kind of changes your perspective, doesn't it?

"But isn't that my job as a mom?" you might ask. It seems like it ought to be because we do it so well! However, it's a complete waste of our time and energy. It accomplishes nothing, and its fruit is anxiety. The Bible shows us the futility of this idol in Luke 12:25: "Who of you by worrying can add a single hour to your life?"

So how do we stop worshiping our circumstances? How do we stop worrying? Matthew 11:28–30 gives us our marching orders. "Come to me, all you who are weary and burdened, and I will give you rest. Take my yoke upon you and learn from me, for I am gentle and humble in heart, and you will find rest for your souls. For my yoke is easy and my burden is light." We often think of this verse for when we're physically weary, emotionally tired, and just plain-old worn out. But notice God says, "Come to me, all you who are weary and *burdened*" (emphasis added). It's the word "burdened" that we often skip over. We're burdened when we're worried.

So the first thing we need to do is come to God. Use our time and energy to talk to Him about our concerns. Turn our worries into prayer. Then trust that He can do far more with them than we can. Remember, He's all-powerful, all-knowing, and omnipresent—He's everywhere! You are none of those things. Allow your soul to rest by placing your worries in God's hands.

Practically, after you do that, get moving. Exercise is a God-given anti-anxiety treatment. When your worrisome thoughts want to creep back in, picture yourself handing them back to God, take a few deep, cleansing breaths, and move on with your day.

Identity

Your personal identity—how you see yourself—is initially formed by your upbringing and your life experiences. If those around you supported and encouraged you and you feel unconditionally loved by God, you probably have a healthy identity. If those around you said and did things that made you doubt your worth and if you think you're a disappointment to God or others, you probably struggle with your identity.

Healthy or unhealthy identity, we all easily fall into the world's trap of defining ourselves by people and things. Without realizing it, we can define ourselves by our job title, our spouse's job title, the neighborhood we live in or don't live in, the car we drive or don't drive, the money we make or don't make, and our kids' hair color, education, jobs, their good and bad choices—yes, even our adult kids' choices.

The world uses these things to give value to people. We live in a judgmental society that looks at people, sizes them up, and slaps a label on them. It's easy to be concerned about what people think because many people will carelessly express what they think. However, we have to reject those evaluations. We have to use a different measuring stick for defining our value. We must derive our identity from our Creator and what He says about us.

Psalm 139:13–14 (ESV) shows us the intentionality of our

creation. "For you formed my inward parts; you knitted me together in my mother's womb. I praise you, for I am fearfully and wonderfully made. Wonderful are your works; my soul knows it very well."

You were designed by your Creator. Not only that, but in order to have a personal relationship with you, your Creator sent his Son, Jesus Christ, to the earth. John 3:16 tells us how much God loves us, reminding us how "God so loved the world, that he gave his one and only Son, that whoever believes in him shall not perish but have eternal life."

What do you believe about your relationship with God? Do you believe He loves you unconditionally? If we're honest, too many of us believe He loves us *only if we do all the right things*. We've been affected negatively by significant relationships that practiced conditional love. This is when we only experience love when we make the other person happy or do things their way. God's not like that. There's nothing you can do to make God love you more and there's nothing you can do to make God love you less.

Society is fickle. People are imperfect. The circumstances of life change all the time. Don't base your identity on any of those changing things. Base it on your unchanging God and kick the identity idol right out of your life.

Control

Author and speaker Paul Tripp says, "I'm increasingly persuaded that there are only two ways of living: 1) trusting God and living in submission to his will and his rule, or 2) trying to be God. There's little in between. As sinners we seem to be better at the latter than we are at the former!"[10]

Those are some pretty strong words, and most of us would react by saying, "I've never tried to be God!" However, our actions indicate differently. We too easily leverage our words and even use nonverbal communication to try to move those around us in a certain direction. Most of us struggle with the idol of control to some extent. If we're honest, we liked the control part of parenting. It was easier that way. The older our kids got, the more control we needed to hand over to them, and the harder parenting became.

Now that our kids are adults, control is not a part of the game anymore at all, yet we still give a lot of time and energy to this idol. Control raises its ugly head when we try to be the Holy Spirit in someone else's life. We know we struggle with control when our happiness is determined by whether things occur according to our plans or desires. If things not going your way disrupts your God-given joy or makes you question God's sovereignty, then you struggle with the idol of control.

> Do I really trust that God is sovereign and everything is under His control? Do I believe He can do a better job making things happen than I can?

Like identity, the root of control comes down to what we think about God. Do I really trust that God is sovereign and everything is under His control? Do I believe He can do a better job making things happen than I can? Do I believe that God is in control even when things are falling apart in my life? The answers to these questions give insight to the places we tend to think wrongly about God. They uncover the lies we believe about ourselves and God.

Control is often carried out incognito. Watch out for these temptations:

- Resist the urge to hint at your adult children to start giving you grandchildren—this is passive-aggressive control.
- Resist the urge to make your spouse or kids feel guilty for choosing something other than what you would choose—this is manipulative control.
- Resist the urge to work to get your way by telling only part of a story—this is deceptive control.
- Resist the urge to react with fear when things don't go your way—this is panic control.

Healing from the idol of control occurs when we can confidently live out Proverbs 3:5–6 (ESV): "Trust in the LORD with all your heart, and do not lean not on your own understanding. In all your ways acknowledge him, and he will make straight your paths." You and I have to trust that God is in control. We don't know or always understand His ways, but we can trust that He is working for the good in our life and in the lives of our loved ones.

Envy

I love Instagram. This and Facebook are my two favorite modes of social media. I'm challenged by some of the authors and bloggers I follow as well as dear friends who are strong in their faith. Sometimes God uses a simple quote, Scripture, video clip, or honest sharing to challenge, motivate, or even change my thinking.

However, they can both also be my downfall. If I'm not careful, they can tickle my tendency to compare. This is the essence of the Perfection Infection. It raises its ugly head when we have unrealistic expectations of ourselves and when we unfairly compare ourselves to others. Social media makes it easy to do both of those.

What we must remember is that we're only seeing the "highlight reels" of other people's lives while we live out the "behind the scenes" reels of our life. Every family has pain. Every family has struggles. When we forget that or get sucked into the highlight-reel lie, we become entangled with the idol of envy and jealousy.

Jealousy raises up when we say, "Lord, why are You blessing them and not me?" or "It's not fair that I should struggle with this hardship when it seems things are easier for them." Our hearts so easily long for what we don't have. We slip into discontentment, blinding us to the blessings we have.

In the empty nest season of life, this can particularly become a challenge when

. . . we see other families celebrating their child's graduation from college and ours has dropped out.

. . . we see another family's child walking strongly in faith while ours is wandering in a spiritual desert.

. . . other people's sons and daughters have weddings while we're still waiting for our turn to be the mother of the bride or groom.

. . . another's child got a promotion and ours is underemployed.

. . . it seems others are physically aging better than we are.

. . . our marriage has failed while others seem to thrive.

. . . it appears that other empty-nesters around us are taking trips or early retirement and look to be set up better financially than we are.

The idol of envy is sneaky, and we rarely identify it immediately. We lick our wounds and feel sorry for ourselves, justifying our feelings and not realizing how tangled up and distracted from the important things in life we've become. This is one idol we must let go of starting today.

Success

When it comes to parenting there are no guaranteed outcomes. There's no formula that says, "If you do A plus B you'll get C." Too often we think that if we do all the right things our child will turn out a certain way.

In an online article, Paul Tripp says,

> We think that if we do our part, our children will become model citizens. We tend to approach parenting with a sense of ownership, that these are our children and their obedience is our right.
>
> These assumptions pave the way for our identity to get wrapped up in our kids. We begin to need them to be what they should be so that we can feel a sense of achievement and success. We begin to look at our children as our trophies rather than God's creatures. We secretly want to display them on the mantels of our lives as visible testimonies to a job well done.[11]

Ouch. That hurts, doesn't it? It's such a good reminder that our kids' jobs are not to make us feel good about ourselves.

Proverbs 22:6 tells us to "Start children off on the way they should go, and even when they are old they will not turn from it." One of the hardest thing about this verse is that it doesn't say the length of time between the first part of this verse and the second part. For many it is dozens of years. Also, while Proverbs is a book of wisdom, a proverb is not always a promise, but rather a conventional truth stated in general terms.

Psychology supports this biblical statement. There is a high probability that you will return to what you know best. Good or bad. We are creatures of habit and what is most familiar is likely what you will return to unless you learn something else in its place. Further supporting this, in an interview about his book *Love and Respect in the Family*, Emerson Eggerichs said, "When I parent God's way, it increases the probability . . . the odds . . . by creating the most loving environment, that my children will then choose my faith and my values. However, there is no absolute guarantee."

This is one thing I was struggling with when our son called to tell us his girlfriend was pregnant. I was embarrassed. I was worried about what people would think. The trophy on the mantel of my life fell off. When we struggle with this idol, we make their behavior about us. Our success. Our reputation. We take their behavior personally, causing us to fight with them instead of fighting for them.

Paul Tripp also says,

Whenever parenting is reduced to our hard work, the child's performance, and the reputation of the family, it becomes very hard for us to respond with selfless faithfulness in the face of our child's failure.

God-ordained moments of ministry will become moments of angry confrontation filled with words of judgment. Instead of leading our needy child to Christ once again, we'll beat them with our words. Instead of loving, we'll reject. Instead of speaking words of hope, we'll condemn. Our feelings will be flooded much more with our own embarrassment, anger, and hurt than with grief over our wayward child's standing with God.[12]

In essence, the idol of success causes us to be ineffective as a parent. Even as an adult, our kids still need us to be a good leader. One of the best ways we can lead them well is by responding to them with love, truth, and grace rather than reacting in anger, judgment, and rejection. If we do the heart work to deal with this idol, our relationship with our kids will be so much healthier.

Clear Out the Clutter

Idols clutter our heart. They keep us tangled up spiritually and emotionally, stealing our focus and energy on the life-giving parts of relationship. The only way to clear the clutter is to confront these idols head-on.

Admit to God what's in your heart (don't worry, He won't be surprised), apologize for defining yourself by anything other than Him, receive His forgiveness, and walk in freedom. You'll be tempted to pick up the idol at times, so you'll have to maintain your freedom with those same steps when you do.

This kind of heart work helps us live out Romans 12:18, which gives us these wise words: "If it is possible, as far as it depends on you, live at peace with everyone." Not only that, but the peace you will experience with a cleaned-up heart will carry you through both the good and the challenging parts of the empty nest season of life.

Truth for Today:

"Come to me, all you who are weary and burdened, and I will give you rest. Take my yoke upon you and learn from me, for I am gentle and humble in heart, and you will find rest for your souls."

Matthew 11:28–29

Take the Next Step:

Take some time to clear out the clutter in your heart this week. Confess your idols to God, ask for His forgiveness. apologize for defining yourself by anything other than Him, receive His forgiveness, and walk in freedom.

Talk with God:

Lord, too often I worship other things more than You. Help me identify anything that clutters up my heart and keeps me from putting You first. Help me let go of the things that hold me back from what You have for me in this next season of life. In Jesus' name, amen.

Part 2

HOLD ON!

"Be alert, be present.
I'm about to do something brand-new.
It's bursting out! Don't you see it?"
Isaiah 43:19 MSG

Chapter 7

GRAB HOLD OF YOUR NEW MISSION FIELD

"I don't want to go to Myrtle Beach with the family, I want to go to Aunt Jill and Uncle Mark's for spring break." Our niece made that surprising announcement to her parents several months before their spring break. They weren't sure she was serious, but she was adamant. They reached out and asked if it was possible for her to stay with us for a week. We replied that we'd be happy to have her. Her spring break visit was the beginning of seeing the possibilities of our new empty nest mission field.

You've spent twenty-some years raising children. In my case and maybe in yours, thirty-some years! Now what do you do with yourself?

Let's go back to our verse from Ecclesiastes 3:6 (MSG):

"There is a right time to hold on and another to let go." We've begun to understand the need to let go. Now it's time for us to explore the first half of that verse. Once we let go, what do we need to grab hold of? There's a whole world out there that desperately needs you. In the next few pages, we're going to explore how to grab hold of our new mission field.

It's Bursting Out

As we set out on our journey to the full life, let's jump over to a couple of other books of the Bible for some direction. Our first stop will be at what might be a familiar verse in the book of Jeremiah. "'For I know the plans I have for you,' declares the LORD, 'plans to prosper you and not to harm you, plans to give you hope and a future'" (29:11).

Although this promise was given to the people Israel, it reveals God's character and heart for His people. Notice it doesn't say, "For I know the plans I have for you until you raise your family." Nope. It says, "For I know the plans I have for you." "Plans" is plural. He doesn't just have one plan for us. He has *more*! The word "prosper" means to thrive or to flourish. He is a good God with good plans for us. He wants what's best for us. His plans are hope-filled and yet-to-come. This means we have something to anticipate. There are things He's likely not yet revealed to us. *Ooh*, I love knowing that there's something around the corner!

If you're familiar with Jeremiah 29:11, it's likely that you stop there, since that's the verse that's quoted most often.

However, let's go on to verses 12 and 13: "'Then you will call on me and come and pray to me, and I will listen to you. You will seek me and find me when you seek me with all your heart.'"

When we call on Him and pray to Him, He will listen. Not He *might* listen. He *will* listen. As we launch into a season of life where the house feels empty and you're yearning for someone to pour your heart out to, God is listening. Then He promises us that if God's people seek Him with all our heart, they will find Him. What wonderful promises these are!

Aren't you glad you're now aware of those pesky idols we just talked about? The more you clean out your heart, the more room there is for God and His ways and His assignments. That's what He means by *when you seek Me with all your heart*. He wants us to abide in Him. We have hope and a future that includes thriving, flourishing, and abiding. He wants us to talk to Him and to make our whole heart available to Him. This encore season of life is not leftovers. It's the main course! You're now in a place where you have the freedom to be used in some ways that weren't possible when you were raising a family.

Let's go to our second stop and move one book back in our Bible to the book of Isaiah. Isaiah 43:18–19 to be specific. "Forget the former things; do not dwell on the past. See, I am doing a new thing! Now it springs up; do you not perceive it? I am making a way in the wilderness and streams in the wasteland." Whoa. Those are some powerful words for some empty nest moms who are feeling a little lost right now.

Of course, God doesn't want us to forget the cute things our kids did or the fun stories that get told at family gatherings. What He does want for us is to not miss the present or the future because our eyes are on the past. This would be akin to driving your car to the grocery store while only looking in the rearview mirror. Sounds silly, doesn't it? We couldn't get to our destination if we did that. Well that's the same way with this encore season of life. My favorite translation of verse 19 is from *The Message*: "Be alert, be present. I'm about to do something brand-new. It's bursting out! Don't you see it?" I love the excitement and energy in those words. I love how they match up with the Jeremiah 29 verses and reaffirm the promise that our hope-filled future includes thriving, abiding, and anticipating something brand-new. God is at work, and our job is to look where He's working, pay attention to what He's doing, and join Him there.

Who Needs You?

There's a big world out there with more needs than anyone could ever count. Some of those needs match up with your passions, talents, or availability. Who needs you? There are so many people who need your listening ear, your helping hand, your experience, knowledge, and wisdom. Not seeing them? Let's take a tour of the empty nest mission field.

Other moms

There's a reason that MOPS groups (Mothers of Preschoolers) have Mentor Moms in their leadership organizational plan. Mentor Moms have "been there, done that." They bring wisdom and experience that only surfaces after someone's made it to the other side. There's a reason that chapter 2 in the book of Titus implores the older women to teach the younger women. They need what we have!

Younger women need hope. They need to know that they won't be potty-training forever. They need you to laughingly reassure them that when your son or daughter graduated high school they weren't still throwing food off the high chair! They also need the hope God's words bring. What young mom could you text a prayer to right now? Or a Bible verse? Or just a quick note to let her know you're thinking of her?

Younger women need help. They need to be able to run to the grocery store without a cart full of kids. When they're sick or have a newborn, they need someone to think of them with a quick phone call from the store asking if there's anything they need. They need help folding laundry. They need date nights with their husbands. Single moms need an occasional break from the kids or someone to show up with dinner . . . just because. Is there a single mom you could adopt and serve? An at-home mom you could relieve once a week or once a month? A working mom you could make a meal for? Would you consider hosting a neighborhood moms' night out at your home centered around a study that can bring them hope? (Check out

Real Moms . . . Real Jesus; *Better Together*; *No More Perfect Moms*; *No More Perfect Kids*; or *No More Perfect Marriages.* These each have a leader's guide to help you lead a discussion, and the last four have free online videos available at www.NoMorePerfect.com and www.BetterTogetherBook.org.)

Younger women need wisdom. When my marriage was going through a hard season, it was the words of a seasoned mom that let me know I wasn't alone. When I shared my heart with Marilee about navigating our son's mental health struggles, her hard-earned knowledge and wisdom were exactly what I needed. Who needs to hear your story?

Younger women need truth. So many of them don't know Jesus and don't understand that they're designed to do life with the God who created them. Some of the above resources mentioned are designed to help introduce moms to the God who loves them. Who could you build a relationship with who needs to know Jesus? Who could you invite out to coffee and get to know?

Younger moms need to be seen. They need to know someone cares. They need to know that someone understands that doing seven loads of laundry in two days is a valuable achievement. They need to know they're not invisible and all alone in this world.

If you don't have grandkids, what if you "adopted" a family who lives far away from their extended family? You'd minister to the mom, dad, and to the kids. Look around at work, in your neighborhood, at church, and in your family. Look for moms' groups or MOPS groups in your community that need Mentor Moms. Luke 10:2 reminds us that "The harvest is plentiful, but the workers are few." Grab hold of the mission field of moms all around you!

Youth

While I was writing this chapter, I was texting with one of my college-aged nieces, encouraging her through a tough time. Sometimes it's easier to talk to your aunt than your mom and dad. I certainly prayed for my own teens and college-age kids to have wise adults to process life with—youth sponsors, pastors, friends, and family—now it's my time to be that in the lives of young adults around me. I have the time, experience, and knowledge to help them.

When our other niece spent spring break with us, she just needed to be seen. She was one of four kids and was feeling lost in the midst of a big, busy family. We talked, shopped, and played double solitaire until we were sick of it. We got our nails done (her first time) and took her to get a haircut (her request). While she was here, she and I started making a latch hook pillow that ended up being a much bigger project than we thought it would be. We've worked on it on several other visits she's made. My goal is to get it done before she goes to college!

Youth may not be your thing and that's okay. Honestly, they're not mine either. I love working with adults, teaching and sharing with peers and those who are past the crazy adolescent emotions. Yet I've tried to make myself available for whatever or whomever God connects me with. Occasionally God asks us to step out of our comfort zone to grow us. Is there a teen around you that could use a listening ear? Some words of encouragement? Ask God to help you see with His eyes.

Your kid's friends

Evan was planning to celebrate his thirtieth birthday with friends at an all-inclusive resort in Mexico. He asked us to come, but it was not a good time for us financially. I had just stepped down from my CEO position at Hearts at Home and we had lost over half our income in that transition. I was launching as an entrepreneur and we didn't yet have consistent revenue streams set up, so we told him that while we wanted to be there to celebrate with him, we just couldn't afford it.

He'd accept that answer for a week or two and then he'd start asking again if we could come. We'd give him the same answer—we wanted to be there but just didn't have the money.

We finally asked him why it was so important for us to be there and he said he really wanted us to come meet some of his friends; these were his gay friends that we didn't know because he lived so far away.

This wasn't just a birthday party—this was a mission field right in front of us that we had not even seen. This was a bridge-building opportunity to love and be the hands and feet of Jesus. We had to figure out a way to honor Evan's request. We moved money around, went without a summer trip we had planned, and made Mexico happen. We're so glad we did!

We loved our time with Evan and his friends. We relished being with our boy who lives so far away. We enjoyed getting to know his friends and hearing their stories. Not only that, we also appreciated the restful break in a beautiful location.

Sometimes your mission field may be right in front of your eyes. Pay attention to who's around you and the opportunities you have to make a difference. It just might surprise you!

Aging parents

In the midst of writing this chapter, I went home to Indianapolis to spend some time with my parents. I suggested that I could help them with their taxes, but it was more than that. I needed to spend time with them and they needed to spend time with me.

If you're still lucky enough to have your parents, they may be part of your empty nest mission field. You may need to help them secure housing that works better for their limitations. You may need to accompany them to doctor appointments. You may need to help them with projects they used to be able to do, but no longer can manage on their own.

On my recent trip home there were three things that struck me while I was there:

1. *Just because help isn't requested doesn't mean help isn't needed.* Mom and Dad didn't ask for help. They rarely do. I just knew it was time to make myself available. Once I was there, they found all kinds of things they

needed help with (like putting away Christmas decorations in the attic two months after Christmas!).

2. *We have to schedule the important.* The urgent things will always keep us busy while the important sits and waits. We have to put the important relationships on the calendar and make them a priority.

3. *Older people don't want to be a bother, but they have needs.* For instance, my dad prides himself in still doing his own taxes at age eighty-four. He's very capable of still doing so; however, it just takes him longer. I helped him categorize and add up tax-deductible expenses, sort and organize receipts, and get things ready for him to do his taxes. If your parent is still capable, don't take away their independence, but rather help them maintain it by assisting as you can.

Aging parents won't be here for forever. Sometimes caring for them is a thankless job and even more difficult if a role-reversal happens and you become their caretaker. They may even be living with you. However, thinking of this opportunity as a mission field can be just the perspective needed to persevere and stay in a positive frame of mind.

Neighbors and friends

My friend Becky has been helping me for over ten years. She's an empty nest mom of one son in his midthirties, and fully committed to "the ministry of availability." Becky was a stay-at-home mom when she was raising her son and she has continued to be a stay-at-home wife in her encore season of life. Let me tell you, she is one busy lady. Becky mentors, encourages, helps, cares for, loves on, and prays for so many.

When I was still raising my family, Becky used her empty nest availability to help me with whatever I needed help with. Seriously, she would say just about monthly, "Let's get a date on the calendar for me to come help you." Help with what? you might ask. Anything I needed! Fold laundry, clean up my kitchen, reorganize a room, get ready for company, cook, clean, sort photos for scrapbooks, or make a photo collage for a graduation party. You name it, she did it. Of course, I had to be willing to accept the help, and I was! Now that I'm not mired down in the everyday challenges of raising a family, I've been able to return the favor on occasion. I've also offered to do the same for other friends who have needed practical help like that. If you love to help people get projects done, this is a great way to bless others.

Maybe you're not a get-in-there-and-get-your-hands-dirty type of person, but you love to write notes of encouragement to others. What if you got serious about sending someone a handwritten note every week? What if you started a card ministry and asked God to show you who needed encouragement sent their way? Maybe you are a prayer warrior. What if you pulled together an organized system for praying for others and spent precious time on your knees?

You need to operate on the empty nest mission field in a way that's true to who you are and how God created you to be.

Don't try to be anyone other than yourself, but don't keep to yourself. There's a world out there that needs you!

The bungee-cord mission field

As I write this chapter, two of our grandkids and their parents are living with us right now. Our son-in-law Matt took a new job in our community. They were living a little over an hour away, so this job transition required them to sell their home. They asked if they could live with us in their transition.

Matt and Anne have stood on their own two feet since they got married twelve years ago. Other than occasional help watching their kids while they chaperone trips (Matt's a youth pastor), they've needed little from us. Mark and I look at this short-term opportunity as a unique mission field to really have special time with our daughter, her husband, and two of our grandkids.

Matt and Anne's house sold, but for less than they hoped. Now they need to build their down payment back up to buy a new home. It looks like they may be here for up to a year. We could look at that negatively (we miss our quiet empty nest life) or positively (we have a unique opportunity we can make the most of).

We do miss our quiet life. I'd be lying if I didn't admit that. Yet it's not forever and we're glad we can help. If they didn't live with us, they could live in an apartment for a season and it would just take them longer to get into a house. However, we have the room and we're willing, so we're helping them get into another house more quickly.

We've done the same with four of our five kids at one time or another. Erica, Kendall, and Marie lived with us when Kendall transitioned out of the army. Evan stayed with us for a month or so after his divorce and before he moved cross-country to California. Nicolai has been in and out a couple of times with his mental health challenges. Austin, our youngest, is the only one who hasn't bungeed back after launching. He's only been out a year sooo . . . we'll see!

Bungee-cord kids can put a cramp in your style for sure. Mark and I have honestly grown to love our empty nest life. It's so much easier to take care of our home with only two people making the messes. Laundry is a once-a-week task instead of daily. Our grocery bill is half of what it used to be. We can watch whatever we want on television and chase each other around naked if we want to (oops . . . did I really just say that?).

However, bungee-cord opportunities have presented themselves and we've decided to make sacrifices in order to engage that mission field. I've never known anyone to go on the mission field without making sacrifices. Missionaries leave behind friends and family. Depending on where they serve, they might forfeit the basic comforts of life. They sacrifice financially, giving up well-paying jobs to live on ministry support. The bungee-cord mission field of parenting requires some sacrifices as well.

If you decide to engage the bungee-cord mission field, it's beneficial to have some guiding principles. Some of this will overlap with those we talked about in chapter 5, helping your child transition through the messy middle, but others are more unique to the bungee-cord situation. We found these helpful.

Help without enabling. If the reason your child wants to live at home for a season of time is to catch their breath financially in between jobs or to transition from one thing to the next, you're probably helping. If the reason your child wants to live at home is because he or she can't keep a job, can't manage their money, or can't stay off drugs or alcohol, you're probably enabling. After several months of staying with us in a transition, our daughter Erica said to us, "If we stay any longer, you'll just be enabling us to not be responsible." We were glad she said it before we had to!

Collect rent. Adults have to pay for their own housing wherever they live. That's the way life works, even if they live with Mom and Dad again. Consider the context of the situation in deciding how much they need to pay. Feel free to barter some household responsibilities in exchange for some of the rent but require them to pay something financially each month. They're contributing to the costs, so they can contribute to paying for the costs.

If they're living with you while job hunting, work out a reasonable time frame for their next step in finding employment. They may have lost their job in a downsizing situation, but if it takes longer than a month or two to find a new job, make sure they understand you expect them to be working at a less-than-ideal job in the meantime (fast food, retail, pizza delivery, something-to-bring-in-some-money).

Require a share of chores. They can help take out the trash, mow the yard, clean the house, and scrub the toilets. After all, they're using all of those things while they live with you. One family we know also requires church attendance for any kid living back at home. It doesn't have to be Mom and Dad's church, just regular attendance somewhere.

Allow for personality differences. Anne and Matt are content with clutter, and Mark and I aren't. We've decided they can keep their bedrooms in whatever condition they choose, but our shared living areas need to be picked up regularly. Sure, a six-year-old and an eight-year-old have their crayons, crafts, and toys all over the place. That's to be expected. However, we ask them to pick up every night before they go to bed so we stay on top of things. I also cleared out a drawer in the kitchen, and any papers/mail/things I find on the kitchen table or counters, I just pop in their drawer. This allows me to keep my counters cleared (which decreases my stress level—tell me I'm not the only one!) and allows them to still find the things that are theirs.

Put everything in writing. Doing this helps clarify expectations on both ends and gives you something to refer to when agreements aren't being kept. You may even put in writing that you expect them to carry their weight of chores cheerfully and without being asked. Sounds silly, but there's a big difference between having to remind people of what they need to do and dealing with them mumbling under their breath and having them just carry their weight responsibly.

Do monthly family check-ins. How are we doing? Is there anything we need to talk about? Is there any way we're frustrating each other? After a month or so, we decided to prepare and eat meals independently. Mark and I cook for ourselves. Matt and Anne cook for their family. It's just easier. Sometimes we eat at the table together and sometimes we don't. It's okay either way.

Ask for what you need in the moment rather than waiting for a monthly check-in. Sometimes I find myself stewing about cleaning up the kitchen after someone else. When that happens, I tell myself, "I can stew or clue." Clue others in to something they need to attend to, that is. What's important to me isn't important to others, so I need to ask for what I need. If I want them to wipe down the stove after they cook something, I may need to ask for that. It seems logical, but different people have a different level of "clean" and what bothers them. Asking in the moment keeps your heart from getting all tangled up in bitterness and frustration.

Stand by your agreements. If agreements aren't being kept, revisit them and offer a warning. If things continue to be difficult, give a thirty-day eviction notice in writing. This protects you should you ever need to call for legal assistance in requiring a family member to leave. It sounds terribly terse and cold, but I've known of a family or two who have needed to go this route.

The Mission Field of Grandkids

Many empty-nesters who have grandkids will tell you they are surprised at how busy they are. This has been a surprise to Mark and me as well. In one season when we helped three of our kids move within three months' time, I said to Mark, "Think about this. If each of our kids or grandkids needed us just once every other month, that would take up every single weekend." No wonder we were feeling tugged in so many different directions! Of course, we can't make every request happen, but we try our best to help and stay connected in whatever way we can.

If the grandkids come along, they are going to need you. Even if they don't act like it (particularly as they get older), they still need you. The empty nest season of life offers a front-row seat on the mission field of grandkids.

Grandkids need your encouragement. They need to know that you love them no matter what and that you're one of their biggest cheerleaders. They need to hear, "You can do it," and "I believe in you," and "You're a great kid" as much as possible. Mom and Dad are knee-deep in parenting—they're tired and overwhelmed at times. They're also trying to find that balance between addressing issues and affirmation. Any amount of affirmation Grandma and Grandpa can provide is a gift!

Grandkids need your time. They need you to listen. To teach them how to do things their mom and dad may be too busy to do. My girls sewed with their grandmother. Even though she lived over two hours away, she helped alter their prom dresses.

Erica designed and sewed her own dress one year, and she and my mom worked together to make that happen. Sewing was not my thing, but Grandma loved it and was good at it!

Grandkids need your help. Last summer I helped then seven-year-old Rilyn with her times tables. She was having a rough time in math, so we worked with them over the phone, when she visited, and through Messenger Kids on the computer. It became our own project for the summer. You are support staff in your grandkids' lives. Look for ways you can help.

Grandkids need your support. If you live close enough, it means the world to them to have their grandma and grandpa in the audience for their school program or sports event. If you're too far away to attend in person, asking to see a video or watching over Facetime can let them know you care and support them in what they're doing.

> So many people have said, "I am the person I am today because of my grandma. She never stopped praying for me."

Grandkids need your prayers. Don't underestimate the power of prayer. I've heard so many stories of people who have said, "I am the person I am today because of my grandma. She never stopped praying for me." One of the most important things you can do is stand in the gap for your grandkids. Pray for their future spouse. Pray for their integrity. Pray for their character. Pray for their decisions. Pray for their schooling. Whatever concerns you have, lift them up in prayer. Prayer is the most important work we have as a grandparent!

Bonding with our grandkids is important. Even if you don't live near your grandkids you can still bond with them. I remember the day we moved away from our kids' grandparents like it was yesterday. My husband and I, our two-year-old daughter and six-week old son were relocating three hours away, allowing Mark to attend Bible college full-time. My mother cried as we said our goodbyes. She was just sure that her grandkids wouldn't know her. In time, however, she and Dad bonded with each of our kids, even at a distance.

Here I am thirty-one years later wanting to make a difference in my grandchildren's lives. I want to be an asset to them, providing a listening ear, a welcoming heart, and possibly a safe place for them to emotionally land when life gets hard. I want to help introduce them to the world around them as well as the faith that will sustain them.

I'm applying my mom and dad's well-lived wisdom as well as paying attention to how other grandparents are connecting intentionally with their grandkids. I've found both practical strategies and positive perspectives to be helpful. Let's take a look at both, starting with the practical strategies first.

Intentionally stay connected

My mother grandmothered from a distance before there was Facetime, social media, or even email. She used the phone, mail, and personal visits. When our children were young and not yet readers, she signed all her cards and notes with a stick-figure picture of herself (she had permed curly hair and always drew a stick figure with curls). When they would open up a card from Grandmother, the kids always knew who it was from because of that drawing. As a toddler, our third child would point to the stick figure and say, "La La La," her nickname for "Grandmother," which is what my mom wanted to be called (hey, she got the three syllables right!).

Use technology to stay connected

If your grandkids are older, find what social media they're using and learn how to use it yourself. Our grade-school grandkids are all set up on Messenger Kids and they communicate a lot with us that way. Even the nonreader sends us stickers and voice memos. We send him stickers and voice memos back. When our son-in-law secured his new job they had to tell their kids they would be moving to a new community. The night our daughter and her husband told the kids, eight-year-old Rilyn hopped on Facebook Messenger to pour her heart out to me. She was upset and couldn't imagine leaving her school and her friends. She couldn't see any good in the news she'd just been told, and she needed someone to listen and offer empathy. I'm so glad we had already laid the groundwork for that conversation to happen!

Engage in their world

Ask about their activities, ask to see their school papers, and show delight when they get their first job. If you live close enough, attend their sports events or choir concerts. My parents often made a two-and-a-half-hour one-way trip for an evening choir concert or school play. The kids loved having them there! Sometimes they stayed over and sometimes they drove back home the same night. If you live too far away to attend, ask for a video or to Facetime during the event so you can still be part of their world!

Set up new traditions

Whether it's Cousins' Weekend, Grammy Camp, or some other tradition you decide to start, make a plan for connecting regularly. Putting your priorities on the calendar first is a good habit to get into so you're investing in the relationships that are most important to you.

Find one-on-one time

I admit with five kids I often parented "the herd." I herded everyone to church, herded them out the door to school, and herded them to the store. I'm trying not to do that with our grandkids. I'm trying to see them as the individuals they are and attempting to figure out what excites them, what they struggle with, and how God has made them unique.

Even from a distance you can interact one-on-one with your grandkids. As they get older, interact with them on social media or call them directly to learn about the things they're doing, who their friends are, and what they're excited about. When you do get to see them in person, try to get some one-on-one time together. One single grandma I know of has taken each of her grandsons, when they turned eight, on a special trip. Almost all of our kids made a cross-country trip with my parents at one time or another to see extended family in Colorado. Sometimes it was just them and Grandmother and Grandad, and sometimes it was them and a sibling. Regardless, it was special time with their grandparents!

I hope these strategies have your wheels turning and you're already thinking of ways you can be intentional. However, there's another side to connecting that's very important. Trying to figure out your place in your child and grandchild's world can sometimes be like navigating a tightrope. That's where the right perspective can make all the difference in the world! Here are eight perspectives I've found to be essential for grandparents:

Watch your expectations.

I once heard someone say, "Expectations are preconceived resentments." Wow, that puts expectations in their place. Too often our disappointment is fueled by unmet expectations. Pay attention to the "ought" and "should" statements rolling around in your head. They're likely fueling any disappointment and discouragement you're feeling. Realistic expectations keep you engaged and content with where your relationship is right now.

There's no grandparent prerogative.

We already talked about this in chapter 3, but it bears repeating again. There's no grandma's prerogative when it comes to grandkids. Their parents are the authority, and you and I need to respect and support them. If you play the "grandma's prerogative" card, you may break trust with your adult child and their spouse and jeopardize future connection with your grandkids.

If you're caring for your grandkids while their parents work, it's okay to have your own house rules, and they may supersede mom and dad's rules while they're in your care. If you're in this situation, you'll want to agree on some guidelines that work for both sides. In this case, it's also valuable to require payment of some amount. Your time is valuable and the service you're providing is huge. Childcare costs money and any adult who has a child needs to carry the weight of that responsibility to some degree. Again, an agreement in writing is important.

This can be a challenging situation to navigate. It's also one where you need to ask yourself if you're helping or enabling. One grandma who had watched her grandkids for several years and then stopped said, "I'm a much better mom to my daughter and grandmother to my grandkids now that I'm not caring for them every day."

Don't take their action (or inaction) personally.

If your preschool-aged grandchild Facetimes all of fifteen seconds with you and then heads off to another activity, that's normal. If your teenage grandson doesn't call you back or respond to your text, that's also normal. It's not about you, so don't make it about you. Recognize that life doesn't always happen the way you think it should. Allow for life context (a busy season, an immature understanding of relational connection, and so on) and imperfect relationships.

No shortcuts

Slow and steady is the name of the grandchild bonding game. Staying connected on a regular basis will build trust and strengthen your relationship. When Rilyn messaged me about the moving news, it was because there was already a road paved for communication.

Accept. Replace judgment with love.

There will be things your grandkids' parents do that you don't agree with. There will be choices your grandchildren will make that you won't agree with. Never sacrifice your relationship on the altar of disagreement. Blue hair? Let it go and love. Tattoos? Let it go and love.

Be secure in your own identity in Christ.

Your children's and grandchildren's always-changing choices do not define you; your unchanging God defines you. When I sense the desire to control creeping in, it's usually because my identity in Christ has slipped to second place and I'm using my kids' and grandkids' choices as an identity barometer. My identity is secure in Christ and yours is too! We need to stay in that place!

Influence, but don't control.

Grandparents have years of experience they long to leverage in their kids' and grandkids' lives, but sometimes that desire moves from influence to control. If you and I sit in the control space, we'll alienate the relationships that mean the most to us. Our most important work is praying for changes we believe need to be made. Our marching orders are to love well, encourage, accept, give wisdom when it's asked for, and pray incessantly.

Remember your place.

You are now extended family for your children and grandchildren. Your son or daughter now has a family they must consider ahead of you. This is a hard but important transition for all of us.

The mission field of grandparenting allows us a second chance to influence the life of a child. It's an encore where we become part of the supporting cast. A little bit of intention partnered with right perspectives can forge a special relationship between you and your grandchildren for years to come.

The Possibilities Are Endless

I was dropping our son off at the train station to return to school when I saw my friend Rosie and her daughter, Erica. Rosie was putting her high school–aged daughter on the train to Chicago as well. When I asked where she was ultimately headed, she said

Erica was taking the train to the college in Milwaukee she was planning to attend in the fall. Her daughter needed to attend an event for incoming freshman athletes. Rosie said to me, "As a single mom, I just can't afford to take a day off work to take her to Milwaukee." My heart broke for Rosie and the challenges she has to face as a single mom. I told her that if she needed someone to help her daughter get transitioned to college, just let me know.

A month or so later, I got a call from Rosie. Erica needed to be on campus for orientation, to register for classes, and to meet with the financial aid department. Would I be willing to take her and attend all those meetings for her? "You bet," I responded.

There is a mission field all around you. Now you can see the possibilities God is talking about in Isaiah 43:19 when He says, "Be alert, be present. I'm about to do something brand-new. It's bursting out! Don't you see it?"

Welcome to this beautiful new season of life—grab hold of your new mission field . . . wherever God shows you it is!

Truth for Today:

"Be alert, be present. I'm about to do something
brand-new. It's bursting out! Don't you see it?"

Isaiah 43:19 (MSG)

Take the Next Step:

Reach out to a young mom this week. Offer to
watch her kids, take her to coffee, or simply drop
her a note letting her know she's a good mom.

Talk with God:

*Lord, I want to see what You have for me in this encore season,
but I confess I'm sometimes blind to it. I also tend to minimize
what I have to offer others. Help me see through Your eyes.
Help me reach out to those around me. May I be filled with
anticipation about what You and I are going to do together
in these empty nest years. In Jesus' name, amen.*

Chapter 8

GRAB HOLD OF NEW PASSIONS

We were planning our first visit to see Evan since he'd moved to California. He was living in West Hollywood, and every hotel I was finding in the area was a minimum of $250 a night. That was *not* in our budget. I mentioned my frustration to a friend who suggested I check out Airbnb. I'd never heard of it. She said it's where everyday people rent out their entire apartment or home or a room in their home. I got on the Airbnb website and found an apartment just three blocks from Evan that rented out for $85 a night. Now that was our price. The pictures looked very nice and the reviews were positive, so I booked it.

We loved it. We enjoyed being in a neighborhood, we were within walking distance of the Hollywood Walk of Fame, we could make our own meals in the kitchen, and we had a relaxing place to just hang with Evan since he and his roommate had such a small place. As we settled into our seats on the plane heading home, I said to Mark, "You know, we could do that. We could be Airbnb hosts. We love people. We both love hospitality. We now have two empty bedrooms and we'll have three when Austin gets married. We could use some extra income. Whaddya think?"

Mark's first response was, "Who in the world would ever travel to Bloomington-Normal, Illinois?" "I don't know," I replied. "Maybe the parents of Illinois State University and Illinois Wesleyan University students? People traveling on Interstate 74 or Interstate 55? I don't know for sure, but we could give it a try and see!"

So we did. We checked out the legal side of things, took some pictures, and set ourselves up on the Airbnb site. We had our first reservation within a week. It was a family bringing their high school–aged son to look at ISU. We so enjoyed visiting with them and sharing our home that we were hooked. Over the past two years we've had over a hundred reservations and met some wonderful people from England, Germany, China, South Korea, and from all across the United States. We're just a mile off the famous Route 66 and we've been amazed at how many have stayed with us while traveling Route 66 for vacation (including one couple from England).

More than anything, we've found that hosting Airbnb brings the mission field right into our living room! We don't have to go anywhere; God brings people to us and we're able to share encouragement, laughter, and, when God makes it evident to us, we can share the gospel. We've had 100 percent 5-star ratings and have been deemed Superhosts by Airbnb. It's become a new empty nest adventure for both Mark and me. With our daughter and her family living with us at the moment, we've made our listing on Airbnb silent for now, but as soon as they're out of the house, Mark and I will take a little break to enjoy the quiet and then we'll get our listing live again.

I'm not suggesting becoming an Airbnb host for all empty-nesters. I'm sharing the story to illustrate that the world is your oyster. There are pearls waiting to be found. It's time to find new adventures to work toward and pour yourself into. It's time to grab hold of new passions!

What Is Your "If We Only Had the Money"?

Stretching our income to feed, clothe, educate, and take care of seven people left little for anything Mark and I would have "liked" to do. As our youngest was finishing up college, our kitchen still had the same green gingham wallpaper we'd hung nearly twenty years ago when we bought our then nearly hundred-year-old farmhouse. The front living room was still painted a dusty-rose color with a cutout floral wallpaper border near our eight-foot ceiling. Very nineties decor. We would have qualified for an HGTV makeover of some kind, for sure!

As the kids have aged, they've begun to have an opinion about our outdated home. "Come on, Mom, the green gingham wallpaper has to go," Evan urged. Finally, the day came when we had a little extra to make a kitchen makeover happen. (It helps when your husband's construction business does that for other people, so you don't have to pay for the labor part of it!) The wallpaper was replaced with chocolate-brown paint, the original cabinets were painted, and the countertops were replaced. We still have almond-colored appliances, however, because they were all still working, and we didn't have the money to change those out too. We eventually got around to painting the living room a beautiful beige, saying goodbye to our dusty-rose walls once and for all.

What is your "if we only had the money" dream? Maybe it's not a project at all. Maybe it's doing some traveling, or finding a vacation home, or taking a mission trip, or visiting a child you sponsor. What's been in the back of your head for a while that you just haven't been able to consider until now?

Maybe it's simply paying off debt. You've just survived financially up to this point and now it's time to get financially healthy. So instead of spending money, you want to actually buckle down and improve your finances or increase what you're contributing to retirement or get serious about retirement for the first time (if that's you, you're not the only empty-nesters who are getting caught up).

It could be that you decide to increase your giving, or support a missionary, or sponsor three more kids. One empty nest couple we know have made it their goal to work toward reverse tithing—living on 10 percent of their money and giving away

90 percent! What a unique goal!

Another empty nest mom shared that this is now her season to pursue her family's genealogy. She's learning about her family's heritage and going through her family's pictures and getting them organized. This will be a beautiful gift for the next generation!

> **What project have you longed to do, but didn't have the time, energy, or money for? What's a possibility now that wasn't five years ago? What's been screaming for your attention?**

What project have you longed to do, but didn't have the time, energy, or money for? What's a possibility now that wasn't five years ago? What's been screaming for your attention? What have you hoped to make happen? Is now the time to do it or make next-step plans to work toward it?

What Is Your "Someday"?

We've all said it at one time or another—"Someday I'd like to. . . ." One of mine is, "Someday I'd like to do community theater again." My degree is music education. I love the theater, performing, and the arts. I'd love to do some more of that, although I don't know how realistic that is with our speaking ministry that keeps us on the road much of the spring and fall.

Maybe your "someday" is taking care of yourself. Maybe you've been at the bottom of the priority list for a long time and it's time to change that. My friend Rhonda did that. I first heard her story when she signed up for my Inspire Speaker Course. I'll let her share it in her own words:

At 45, I was finally ready to take control of a lifelong battle with my weight. My knees had begun to ache, and daily nursing home visits to see my mother-in-law gave me a clear picture of what a lack of mobility and poor health could look like in my future. I found a local exercise program through a newspaper article and started doing a "boot camp" class three days a week. Having been a chubby child to an adult peak weight of 222 pounds, movement and exercise had never been an enjoyable part of my life, but this was different. Within a few weeks I was encouraged by the changes I saw. My coach's great workouts, continual support, and encouragement also gave me the mental strength and confidence to know a healthy, fit lifestyle was possible for me.

Reaching out for help was a huge hurdle for me. Health and weight loss had always seemed like something I should have been able to do on my own. But the knowledgeable and compassionate helpers I found at the boot camp, as well as being surrounded by like-minded women in my class, shifted my thinking about seeking outside help.

In addition to making changes in my diet, I also discovered that I needed to work on the mental and emotional pieces of this lifestyle change to ensure my new healthy behaviors would stick. This part was tough. Losing weight and being fit was something I had wanted my whole life, and now I needed to change some of my wrong thinking patterns, as well.

The journey from "before" to "after" is ongoing. Now that I am in my 50s, the lifestyle changes I have made along the way are more important than ever. As my body changes with age, my diet and exercise regimens have had to change, too.

Recently on the latest leg of my journey I have found Functional Medicine and Functional Medicine Health Coaching. Being a health coach is a new career opportunity for me in my "parenthood retirement." Not only am I helping myself continue to stay healthy, now as a health coach I am able to use what I have learned on my own journey to support others along their path to attain their goals. This journey has literally taken my life in an amazing new direction for my empty nest years!

You might "fall" into a new career like Rhonda did after her weight loss journey or a new hobby like we did with Airbnb. You might also have some intentional direction to take. Do you have some "unfinished business" that's been burning in your heart for many years, like returning to finish that college degree you never completed or even started? Maybe you'd like to pursue a graduate degree that would allow you additional career opportunities. Or become a Master Gardener. Or enter your incredible banana bread recipe in the state fair competition. Whatever is on your "someday" list, your encore season of life is the perfect time to make it happen.

By the way, it's never too late. Depending on your age, you could finish a degree and still have ten to fifteen years to work in a new area of employment. Or you could go to school simply to learn. My friend Becky is currently auditing courses in Spiritual Formation from Lincoln Christian University. She will complete the same courses those who earn a degree will, but auditing the classes costs a lot less money and she simply wants to learn and deepen her own spiritual journey.

What's on Your Bucket List?

I'd love to make a trip to the Holy Land someday. I'd love to walk where Jesus walked. I'd love to see Jerusalem. Honestly, it's the only big thing on my bucket list. Mark would also love to go to the Holy Land and he'd like to take an Alaskan cruise. These are both trips we're saving for right now. Who knows how long it will take us to save enough to make the trips, but we've got a goal in front of us we're working toward.

A bucket list is the experiences or achievements you want to have or accomplish during your lifetime. So what's on your bucket list? Skydiving? Traveling somewhere? Visiting all fifty states? Learning to ride a motorcycle?

Go ahead, get out your journal or a piece of paper, and start your bucket list. Here are some questions that will help get you started:

If you had no limits on money or time, what would you do?
Think of something you've always wanted to do but haven't
    yet.
Where would you most like to go? A foreign country? Places
    in this country? Interesting places near your own area?
Think big: What are your greatest goals? Dreams?
Is there anything or anyone you would like to see in person?
Is there anything you would like to achieve?
What experiences do you want to be sure not to miss?
What about moments you would enjoy being witness to
    (e.g., a naturalization ceremony, a graduation)?
"I'd like to try _____."
What are some skills you'd like to learn?
Are there any activities you like to do with other people?
    People you love? Family? Friends?
What do you want to achieve spiritually?
What do you want to achieve with your health?
What do you want to achieve in your finances?
What do you want to achieve in your career?

To Work or Not to Work?

Speaking of career . . . what do you want to do with that? The
question of work may not be a question at all. Your financial
situation may require that you work. Your relationship status
may also require that you work. Or you have a satisfying job you
thoroughly enjoy and have no plans to give it up anytime soon.

However, if you're married and have always been a stay-at-home mom, you can, like my friend Becky, continue to be committed to the "ministry of availability." There are so many possibilities for you to mentor, encourage, help, teach, care for, volunteer, and love on your family, friends, and those around you. Our church has what they call "ministry partners," which are super-volunteers who offer as many hours that would qualify as part-time or full-time positions in the workplace. It's a perfect opportunity for empty-nesters who want to be part of something bigger than themselves but not be saddled with job expectations.

If you still desire to work, but don't have to financially, what about giving entrepreneurship a try? My friend Linda is taking this road. I'll let her share her own story.

As I was approaching the empty nest years I was panicking. I felt like there were so many things that I had missed out on doing with my kids that I started trying to make up for lost time. I even suggested doing crafts with my girls when they were in their junior and senior years of high school. Crazy, right?

I stumbled around in my early empty nest years trying to figure out this new season of life. I volunteered, dabbled in speaking, went on some mission trips to Haiti, and continued to tutor, which is something I'd done for years. Then an idea began to birth in me.

I love baking. I love encouraging. I love the missions

work my husband and I have done in Haiti. What if I blended all three of those passions into a new venture? This is how Num Num Box (www.NumNumBox.com) was birthed! Parents long to send their college students care packages to let them know they're thinking of them but often don't have the time to make that happen. They also want to keep sending encouragement their way. With Num Num Box, I bake the cookies, box them up, pop in a comfort item, a devotion, and send them out. All profits go to support the Haiti missions we love so much as well as a local homeless shelter! I'm still in the early months, but I'm loving the creating process and the possibility in front of me!

I'm on the same journey as Linda. I'm an entrepreneur at heart. I prefer a flexible schedule, a small, nimble team, being my own boss, and not being weighed down with the people challenges that come with large organizations. I'm being true to me in how I choose to work in my encore season of life. It's taken some time to get to a full-time income doing what I love—speaking, writing, teaching, and coaching—but it's been worth it!

Maybe work is just work for you. You show up, do your job, and collect your paycheck. It works for you and you're completely fine doing that until retirement. That's okay, too! This is just a good time to evaluate your work strategy as you launch into this new season of life. Ask God to show you any options that might be in front of your eyes that you're completely missing. Then recommit to what you're doing or start exploring the possibilities of a new direction. Both are valuable next steps to take.

I'm Not Done Nurturing!

A mama's design to nurture doesn't just turn off when her birdies fly away. Most of us still feel we have something to offer. We naturally do the baby sway when standing near a mom who is comforting her child. We're experts at kissing boo-boos and reading nighttime stories. We can make a paper snowflake like no one else! What do we do with all that nurturing still inside us? We have to find opportunities that match up well with our desires. Here are some possibilities to consider:

International college students/exchange students

The call came in unexpectedly from a friend of a friend. A host family for a one-month exchange student program fell through. They needed a host family for one eighteen-year-old boy. Would we be willing? We had two boys, sixteen and eighteen, still at home, so it was a natural fit. We decided to say yes, and Inigo from Spain became part of our family for a month. That was eight years ago. We so enjoyed his time with our family and we still stay in touch with him through social media.

Several years later, a similar situation happened with an Illinois State University international student who needed housing for just a week or so before campus housing became available. Haera became our "adopted daughter," and we became her "American parents" for the four years she was here. We recently celebrated her graduation and sent her off to her first internship in California.

Some empty nest couples and singles love hosting high school exchange students for the nine months they're in this country. This gives them the opportunity to still do the school routine and attend extracurricular activities while influencing and guiding another young life. With our crazy travel schedule, we find college international students are more our thing than high school students. We don't need the daily responsibility of high school exchange programs, but we love the flexible, touch-base-occasionally opportunities that helping international students provides.

If hosting international students sounds like something you might enjoy, a call to your local high school or college can get you started. The students need the nurturing you still have to offer. They need to know someone cares here on this side of the world. They also need an occasional home-cooked meal, help with the practical parts of life (I taught Haera how to drive), and maybe even somewhere to spend the holidays when they just can't afford to go back home.

Nursery worker

Do you love snuggling little ones? Need that baby fix every once in a while? Consider working in the church nursery, or caring for the babies of moms attending a local moms' group, or even becoming a hospital volunteer.

The church nursery is a wonderful place to get a baby fix. You can love them and snuggle them, but you don't have to be up half the night with them! Moms' groups are also a great place to love on some little ones. If you work in the childcare program, your job is to take care of little ones so their mommy can get a break, connect with other moms, and learn something. I speak at many moms' groups, and I also often see mentor moms (who are usually in the room where their program is taking place) walking fussy newborns (who are too small for their moms to be comfortable putting them in childcare) around the room while I'm speaking. This gives the moms a much-needed break and the mentor mom a much-needed baby fix!

Many hospitals use volunteer "baby cuddlers" in their neonatal units. Sometimes they need cuddlers to hold babies whose parents are ill or injured in an accident and are unable to provide early cuddling opportunities that are important for healthy development. Sometimes cuddlers are used for holding babies who are in withdrawal after being born to moms who are addicted to drugs. If your arms still long to hold little ones, there are plenty of them out there to hold!

Sponsor a child . . . or two!

I first learned about child sponsorship when Hearts at Home, the organization I led for twenty-four years, started partnering with Compassion International. Mark and I decided we would sponsor a child that year. We chose Daniel from Honduras because our kids were taking Spanish in school and they could use the practice both reading and writing Spanish (you usually write the letters in English and Compassion translates them, but if you know their language, you can certainly write to them in it!). We started receiving his letters and pictures, which we put on the refrigerator, and began to write him back. We prayed for him, encouraged him, shared truth with him, and told him we believed in him. He was our sponsored child until his parents moved and he left the program. Then we chose Ander, also a young man from Honduras. Ander is still our sponsored child and we're still writing him, praying for him, and encouraging him.

At one of my speaking engagements a mom came up to my book table and shared that Compassion is her way of using her natural nurturing desires in this in-between time of having adult kids but no grandkids. "I sponsor five kids," she said proudly. She continued to share, "I love writing them letters, sending cards, or just using the Compassion app to send a quick note and picture to let them know I'm thinking of them and I believe in them."

Want to sponsor a Compassion child? Use this special link and we'll see how many we can sponsor through this book: www.compassion.com/emptynest![13]

Become a big brother/big sister or a CASA

The Big Brothers Big Sisters program is another way to make a difference in the life of a child. When you're a "Big," you can offer friendship and be a role model for a "Little" who needs a positive adult in their life for a few hours a couple times a month. Play a board game, make crafts, go to the park, help him or her with homework, go to a ball game, do whatever activities your "Little" loves. This allows you to nurture a life that may not have much nurturing otherwise. (To learn more check out www.bbbs.org!)

Kids Hope (www.KidsHopeUSA.org) pairs a church with a public school, and volunteers mentor a child for one hour a week. If your church isn't already involved, you might look into starting and coordinating this partnership. Safe Families (www .Safe-Families.org) is another great organization that allows volunteers to temporarily host children and provide a network of support to families in crisis while they get back on their feet. My sister and her husband are a Safe Family, and they love this ministry. Even getting involved in your local public school can be a natural fit for an empty nest mom after all her years of school involvement with her own kids.

Another option is becoming a Court Appointed Special Advocate. A CASA is a trained volunteer who is appointed by a judge to advocate for an abused or neglected child in juvenile court proceedings. No special background or education is required to become a volunteer. People are needed from all professional and educational backgrounds, all cultures, all ethnicities. After you've been accepted to train as a CASA, you'll learn what you need to know about social services, court proceedings, special needs abused or neglected children have.

This can be a very fulfilling experience for those who want to make a difference in the life of a child. It's not for the faint of heart or super-sensitive mamas because you'll definitely be introduced to a world you're likely not familiar with. However, if you have a heart for the hurting and long to advocate for someone who doesn't have a voice, becoming a CASA volunteer could be a good empty nest opportunity. (Check out www.Casa-ForChildren.org to learn more.)

There are so many possibilities for exploring new passions: teaching Sunday school, children's church, becoming a youth sponsor, scouting, and becoming a hospice or a nursing home volunteer, just to name a few more nurturing options. Keep your eyes open and your heart sensitive to what's going on around you. You're not done nurturing yet, and there are so many needs around you!

The Freedom of the Season

Raising a family is like being a hot-air balloon tethered to the ground. Your life is full and your design is beautiful, but you can't cut the ropes and fly carefree. Once your family is raised, the opportunity to take flight offers so many possibilities.

Maybe we shouldn't call it the empty nest at all; maybe we should call it the open nest, a suggestion from my friend Sue, because it's open for new experiences and new nurturing opportunities. New possibilities are there to explore. Long-held passions ready to pursue. Young lives that still need nurturing. And don't forget to keep asking God what He has for you. His plans may not even be on your radar right now, so stay flexible and sensitive to His leading. You can trust He has a purpose for you in this season of life! Grab hold of it!

Truth for Today:

"Work willingly at whatever you do, as though you were working for the Lord rather than for people."

Colossians 3:23 (NLT)

Take the Next Step:

What's been on your "someday" list that needs to be moved to "now"? Take the next step in moving forward on something you know you've needed to do or something you've always want to do.

Talk with God:

Lord, I've been so focused on my kids that I've forgotten who I am and who You made me to be. Bring those interests, passions, dreams, and desires to the surface of my life. Show me the single next right step to walk toward at least one of those. Keep me looking for what You're doing and recognizing Your invitation to join You there. In Jesus' name, amen.

Chapter 9

GRAB HOLD OF NEW FRIENDSHIPS

Not again! Another close friend—my fifth best friend in twenty years—was moving away due to a work transfer. I wanted to scream, "I don't have time for this! I'm a friendship-for-life girl. I don't want to start all over again!" I've maintained a connection with each of my friends who have moved away, but it's not the same as doing everyday life together. It's not the same as knowing you can just walk into her house and get some sugar when she's out of town.

Maybe you're the one who's moved. Here you're figuring out a new season of life in a new city. This wasn't what you pictured yourself doing. This wasn't a part of your plan and quite honestly, you're tired. You're not sure you have the energy to do it all over again.

By the time your kids are grown you've been doing the "adult friendship" thing for a while. Maybe it's something you've always struggled with. Friendship has been hard, period. You've always felt a little on the outside. Maybe it's something you've never struggled with but now things have changed and you're finding yourself in uncharted waters. Finding and nurturing friendships in the empty nest season of life has its joys and its challenges. Let's dig in to better understand why and what we can do about it.

No More Bleacher-Butt Friendships

When we're raising kids, our friendships are often formed sitting on the sidelines of sports events, helping with school musicals, and behind the scenes at dance recitals. In the early years there are playdates, park visits, and moms' groups where the seeds of friendship are planted, watered, and fertilized as you visit with other moms while the kids are happily off with their playmates.

These natural connecting points for moms disappear in the empty nest years. You're no longer sharing activities with the parents of other kids. You're no longer in the same place at the same time. This means you have to change your friendship strategy. Maybe you didn't even know you had a friendship strategy, but you did . . . by default.

Growing and maintaining friendships will now require a different kind of intentionality. Unless you're working in an office and someone happens to be in the same season of life as you, or you belong to an empty nest small group at church, there will rarely be default opportunities to be around other moms who understand what your world is like. You need that. You need to feel understood. You need to not feel alone. More than anything, you need some people in your tribe to carry you when life is hard and to cheer you on when life deserves a celebration.

The Joys of Empty Nest Friendships

Parenthood retirement, as my friend Rhonda calls it, offers some unique opportunities as it relates to friendship. I asked a group of same-season friends specifically about that and how they've seen the empty nest affect their friendships positively. The first thing mentioned was the fact that you can have uninterrupted conversation! Now that's a gift for sure. No one is interrupting with "Mom . . . *Mom* . . . *MOM*!!!" every five minutes. You can talk, go deeper, and actually keep your train of thought.

One mom mentioned having a little more disposable income. Going to a conference, a retreat (watch for my *Empty Nest, Full Life* retreats), a concert, or even a girls' weekend away seems more financially possible than in the past. I agreed with her as I've experienced that myself. Don't have any of those on your calendar? Invite someone, make plans, and go!

Freedom was mentioned several times. It used to be hard to do things with friends because you had to make so many plans for childcare, meals, school pickup, and so on. Now you can just leave! (If you're like my mom and going to be gone for a few days, you may need to leave a few meals for your hubby, but those are much easier than making plans to feed a whole family in your absence.)

For those who are married, doing more things with couple friends was previously mentioned. You can pick up and leave so much more easily. Go out to dinner more often. Even take trips you could have only dreamed about in the past. Navigating couple friends is something we'll talk about in the next chapter on marriage. For now, let's suffice it to say that if you have couple friends, the empty nest allows for more possibilities to invest in those relationships as well.

If you're widowed, divorced, or never have been married, friendships are even more important because when your nest is empty, it's really empty! You need a strong circle around you so you don't tackle this season solo. You need to be with other women who really do understand what your life is like.

As with any stage of life, friendships let us know we're not alone. They keep us connected to others in the good parts of life and the hard parts of life. Living in relationship with others is the way you and I are actually designed to live. Jesus modeled community. He led the way. We need to take our cues from Him.

You're Not Meant to Do Life Alone

When you study Jesus' adult life, one of the first things you'll notice is Jesus invited each disciple to do life with Him. Jesus saw people as individuals. He reached out to them personally. He invited them into relationship. You and I need to do the same.

Our world is becoming more and more isolated. We push a button in our car to open our garage door, close it with the same button, and retreat into our home or backyard with its privacy fence, often without even glimpsing other people. People don't "neighbor" like they used to. They don't invite others over for dinner. They keep to themselves, pseudo-connecting with others on their phone or computer.

We have to recognize this unhealthy cultural pattern and not get sucked into it. You and I need real community. Face-to-face conversations. Hugs. Laughter. Experiencing fun together. Deep conversations. Prayer. These are the beautiful parts of community we have to fight for. It takes effort, requires risk, and may even necessitate courage.

How much community you need will depend on whether you're an introvert or an extrovert. Introverts are refueled by being alone and extroverts are refueled by being with people. Now this doesn't mean introverts get a pass on community. It just means they need it in smaller doses.

I'm an introvert. I'd much rather have one-on-one coffee with someone than go to a party. I have just a couple of close friends, which is why it's such a big deal when someone moves away. One lunch out with a friend is plenty of community for me for a week—of course that lunch could last hours if we have the time because I like to go deep more than wide. All that is normal for an introvert. My husband is an extrovert. A lively party charges him up, he has many more friends than I do, and he could do lunch with someone different every day and be perfectly fine with it.

You need to know yourself and how to navigate building community in a way that works with how God made you. Identify your people capacity and then be true to yourself. Believe it or not, aging can play a part in this as well. I hear from many fiftysomethings that they're finding they're more tired than their younger selves were. As they age, extroverts can become a little more introverted, not longing for as much social life as in the past. If you're working full-time, it's possible you get to the evening and just don't want to do anything else. That's normal! You and I have to work with our limitations rather than letting them win. For instance, maybe you choose to connect with community over your lunch hour or on Saturday afternoon, or just one evening a week so you have most after-work evenings to yourself. You might mix friendship and exercise with a walking buddy. Make community a priority, but work with your energy level as well as your personality and temperament.

You might even use this book to connect with some new women who understand what your world is like. What if you did an *Empty Nest, Full Life* book study? Invite three to five women who might be interested. Ask them to each invite one other person to join the group. Use the leader's guide in the back of the book to guide conversation. Have each participant read one chapter a week, then gather to discuss it. You'll learn so much from reading the book together and talking about it. You'll find out you're not as alone as you sometimes feel, and you'll learn from each other as you talk about the chapters. Once you're done with *Empty Nest, Full Life*, if the group wants to stay together, *No More Perfect Moms* or *No More Perfect Marriages* would be great follow-up studies because they're appropriate for all ages and stages of motherhood.

Another option would be to start or join a Moms In Prayer group (www.MomsInPrayer.org). They have groups for Grandmothers in Prayer, Moms Praying for Prodigals, and College Praying Moms. I was a part of a Moms In Prayer group when my kids were growing up. This really taught me how to pray and how to turn my worries into prayer. I recently learned that they have these groups for empty-nesters, too!

You still need a moms' group, a community, a tribe. It could be a circle of friends you already have or one you need to build. It could be reigniting old relationships or establishing new ones. What I know for sure is you need other moms and other moms need you. Yes, *you*!

You Have So Much to Offer

I received the invitation to a "My Favorite Things" Christmas party at my friend Lisa's house. I've known Lisa for years but have never known her to have a Christmas party. I put it on my calendar and looked forward to it for weeks. We were asked to bring a favorite appetizer or dessert and three small gifts—no more than $10 each—of our favorite things. When we arrived, I knew only some of the people in the room. We visited for a while, then Lisa invited us to make a plate of food and join her in the dining room. There were about fifteen of us and we crowded around her long dining room table. That's when we learned this party was Lisa's way of celebrating friendship.

Lisa told us she was patterning her party after what Oprah used to do with her "My Favorite Things" show. She began to go around the table one by one handing out small gifts and telling each of us what she appreciated most and what it is we've brought to her life. She told me that I've brought steadfastness to her life. As I've walked through hard times, she's watched me be steadfast and that has helped her. The party ended with our gift exchange when we got to share some of our own favorite things and then we each received one more gift from Lisa (they were paperwhite bulbs with instructions on how to plant them). It was the most thoughtful way to honor friendship I've ever seen!

All of us gathered around her table were her tribe. Now, we weren't all in relationship with each other. The common denominator was Lisa. We'd all shared life with Lisa in some way and she wanted to celebrate what we'd brought to her life. However, most of us were empty-nesters or nearly empty-nesters, and we ended up having an informal moms' group that evening. We shared some of our stories talking about the challenges of kids leaving, navigating the changes at the holidays, and ideas for making the transition smoother.

For each of us, life is a mixture of pleasures and challenges.

Easy and Hard. Painful and Joyful. We all have stories to share and when we share our stories with others, we live out 2 Corinthians 1:3–4 (MSG), which tells us God "comes alongside us when we go through hard times, and before you know it, he brings us alongside someone else who is going through hard times so that we can be there for that person just as God was there for us." Sharing your story helps another mom through her story.

> **For each of us, life is a mixture of pleasures and challenges. Easy and Hard. Painful and Joyful. We all have stories to share.**

Of course, you don't have to share your story like I have on my blog, on a stage, or in a book. You just need to steward your story when God gives you the opportunity to share. Each of us has a story that can encourage others. Each of us can give "a reason for the hope that is in you" (1 Peter 3:15 ESV).

One of the "getting to know you" questions I often ask when I'm visiting with someone I don't know well is, "So, what's your story?" It's a broad question, but I've never had anyone not understand what I'm asking. Sometimes they'll want to clarify: "Do you mean my faith story or my life story?" I tell them either one is fine with me. Usually they'll laugh, look at their watch, and say, "Well, how long do you have?" I encourage them to simply give me their highlights. There are three types of stories we can share: our life story, our faith story, and our experience story. Let's take a look at each of these.

What's Your Story?

When we share the highlights of our life story, we're sharing bits and pieces of our journey in hopes of finding connecting points with the person we're sharing with. This isn't where you share your darkest secrets. It's where you give them a bird's-eye view of the journey that has brought you to today.

Your life story

Here's my story: I grew up in Avon, Indiana, which is a western suburb of Indianapolis. My dad was an English teacher, then a principal, and eventually a superintendent. My mother was a stay-at-home mom until my two sisters and I were in school, and then she got a job as a school secretary. I grew up attending the United Methodist Church with my family. After high school, I attended Butler University and majored in choral music education.

I met Mark on a blind date right before I started at Butler. We got married after my freshman year of college, had Anne, our first child, during my junior year, and Evan, our second, on my college graduation day. Needless to say, Butler mailed me my diploma.

Mark worked for a family business when we married, but he felt called to ministry, so we packed up our little family and moved to Lincoln, Illinois, so he could attend Lincoln Bible College (now known as Lincoln Christian University). I was a daycare provider by day and worked in a dinner theatre by night to make ends meet. When Mark was offered an internship at a large church in Bloomington, Illinois, we moved our family and he commuted to school. Shortly after we moved, Erica was born. I taught piano and voice lessons for fifteen years until our youngest, Austin, was born. By that time, Hearts at Home, the ministry to moms I started, was growing faster than I ever imagined. Several years later, we adopted Nicolai, our son from Russia, bringing us to a grand total of five kids.

Mark was a pastor for twenty years and now owns his own home-remodeling business. Our kids are grown, ranging in age from twenty-three to thirty-four. We just celebrated our thirty-sixth wedding anniversary (which has been hard-earned!), and we have three grandkids who call us Nana and Papaw. Mark still works construction, but he and I now do a lot of work with marriages. We host marriage intensives in our home, run a marriage membership site (www.NoMorePerfectDateNight .com), and we travel to churches leading our No More Perfect Marriages retreats.

Do you see how hearing my story gave you some connecting points you might not have known? If we'd been sitting down having a cup of tea together, it likely would have prompted some questions that could have led to great conversation.

So what about you? Take a few minutes and think about your story. Either in your head, out loud, or in a journal, form a two- to three-minute version that gives the highlights of your journey. Think about the pieces of your story that may connect with another mom in some way: where you grew up, any post–high school education, what you did BK (before kids), adoptive or biological journey, and stage of life now. Hearing someone's story or sharing your story is somewhat like peeking through the window of a house you might want to enter. It lets you come to understand what experiences have formed and shaped someone.

Your faith story

Our journey of coming to know God is another story we can share. This too allows for making unique connecting points. Part of my husband's faith story is that he accepted Christ at a Billy Graham crusade. It's amazing how sharing that one little piece of information opens up conversation with someone who also knows someone who had a life-changing experience because of Billy Graham.

Here's my faith story: I grew up attending church. My family's commitment to church gave me a great foundation of faith. However, as I entered college, I longed for something more. It was a sorority sister who helped me move from religion to relationship. Beth introduced me to contemporary Christian music. The personal connection I sensed in that heartfelt music eventually led me to a personal relationship with Jesus Christ. (I'll share more about what a personal relationship with Jesus Christ is all about a little later.)

When I met Mark, he was a new believer. We've both grown in our faith together throughout our marriage. When I think about my own personal spiritual influences, I'd have to say my

Mom2Mom group, twenty-four years of Hearts at Home conferences, being a part of a Moms In Prayer group, digging into God's Word for wisdom, reading books, having some strong Christian friends, and being in good churches have been essential pieces of growing my faith.

What's your faith story? Take a few minutes to think through how you would describe the path your faith has taken. If you journal, write it down! When you have a chance—maybe over coffee with a new friend—ask about her faith story. Then share yours!

Experience stories

We have our life story, our faith story, and then we have our experience stories. These are life circumstances we've walked through and how God has grown us through those experiences. I've shared some of my experience stories with you in this book. Some of my other experience stories include living on very little money when Mark was in school, doing day care in my home, adopting a child from Russia, having a prodigal child who doesn't share our family's faith, surviving breast cancer, mending our marriage after infidelity, and specific challenges with having a son with multiple mental health diagnoses.

These are the stories I carry with me, asking God daily how He wants me to leverage them for His good. You have these stories too. Maybe you've never thought of them as stories, but they are. In fact, they are what I call your backstories. The ones you carry in your heart but people don't necessarily know about unless you tell them. Some of the life circumstances you've experienced are positive stories that illustrate hope, courage, and faith. Some of the life circumstances you've experienced are painful stories that exemplify redemption, recovery, and restoration. These are sometimes the hardest stories to share, but walking through them ultimately gives us more depth and the potential to be a better friend.

Your outside appearance usually doesn't communicate the circumstances that have shaped you. Neither does someone else's. If I start comparing myself to someone else, I remind myself that there's more to her and to her life than I know; she has a life story, probably a faith story, and most definitely experience stories that have contributed to how she operates in this world. She may look confident and put together on the outside, but I know she's had pain in her life just like I have.

Your stories matter. You have so much to offer to others. Your years of raising a family have produced so much wisdom simply because you've had so many experiences. You also have so much in common with other moms at this place in their life. Let these enrich your current friendships or be a part of planting the seeds of new ones.

"There You Are!"

Not long ago my daughter Anne and I coauthored the book *Better Together: Because You're Not Meant to Mom Alone*. If friendship has always been a struggle for you, that's a book you might want to pick up because it will cover way more than we could ever cover in a chapter. However, we shared in the book the often repeated adage that there are two types of people in this world: those who walk into a room and say, "Here I am" and those who walk into a room and say, "There you are."

Maybe you have all the friendships you feel like you can keep up with. You don't desire to invite any more relationships into your life. Being a "there you are" person doesn't have to start friendships, but it simply allows you to see people. It's caring more about others around you than yourself. There's nothing more isolating than to not feel seen. When you see others, you let them know they matter. Who knows? This may be how God opens your heart up to a new passion to pursue or a person whose path you cross that needs the nurturing you still have to offer.

However, if you're finding friendships to be less than you'd like in your current season, becoming a "there you are" person may help you spark friendship possibilities. Who might you see Sunday at church and invite out for coffee or over for dinner? What neighbor have you never taken the time to know? Is there someone at work you might enjoy getting together with outside the office?

> What neighbor have you never taken the time to know? Is there someone at work you might enjoy getting together with outside the office? Any friendships you need to blow the dust off of and reignite?

Any friendships you need to blow the dust off of and reignite? If you're married, is there another empty nest couple you might invite over for dinner? Who could you see through different eyes? Who could you invite?

Beware of the lies of the enemy that will keep you from inviting. Here are just a few:

Why would she want to go to coffee with me?
I'm sure she has plenty of friends.
She would probably just say yes to be polite. I'm not a good friend anyway, don't string her along. What if she says no and I have to deal with rejection again?

These lies will keep you isolated. They will build fear and anxiety and keep you from building community. They will foster loneliness.

I've had some pretty painful experiences with friends. One friend literally broke up with me. We had lived life together *daily* and then she took me to coffee and told me we couldn't be friends anymore. No explanation why. I still don't know to this day. That's painful, and when those things happen is when the enemy gets in there and starts whispering those lies.

Leading a ministry was also relationally hard for me. Some people I thought were my friends were actually leveraging the relationship for their own benefit. Others were highly critical and I grew weary of the constant carping. I'm sure you've had your fair share of friendship fiascos. So did Jesus. His friend

Judas betrayed Him. His friend Peter denied even knowing Him. His friends who gathered in the garden of Gethsemane to pray with Him fell asleep instead.

Most of us can come up with plenty of rationalizations for why it's okay to be like a turtle, pulling our head inside our shell to block the crazy world out there. It will feel good for a while, but we'll eventually come up empty. When you're one piece in the big puzzle of life, you'll eventually yearn to find some other pieces that connect specifically to you. Keep asking God for wisdom for next steps in relationships. Stay in the game. Find your tribe. The benefits are worth the risks!

No More Lone-Ranger Empty Nest Moms

We have to invest in what's already there, build what's not yet there, and believe wholeheartedly that we'll be a better person because of it. We also have to remember that friendship isn't once and done; it's ever changing. If you are stinging from a friendship fiasco, or a dear friend moving away, or feeling like you don't have a friend in the world, I just want you to know today that you are not alone.

You're in a new season of life with new possibilities. Just like our passage in Isaiah 43:18–19 (MSG) says, "Be alert, be present. I'm about to do something brand-new. It's bursting out! Don't you see it?" Yes, God even has something new for our friendships. Grab hold of that today!

Truth for Today:

"God is our merciful Father and the source of all comfort. He comforts us in all our troubles so that we can comfort others. When they are troubled, we will be able to give them the same comfort God has given us."

2 Corinthians 1:3b–4 (NLT)

Take the Next Step:

Connect intentionally with one friend this week. Send her a text, invite her over, meet her for coffee, or give her a call.

Talk with God:

Lord, I know You're my Friend, but I also understand I sometimes need someone I can touch. Show me the lies I believe that keep me from pursuing community. Help me see those who need to be seen. Give me courage to risk rejection when pursuing new friendships. Is there someone who needs this book, Lord? Show me who that is and prompt me to take action to send her a copy. In Jesus' name, amen.

Chapter 10

GRAB HOLD OF YOUR MARRIAGE

Note: While most of the book has been written with a female audience in mind, this chapter is different. Since marriage takes two, it's written in a way that both husbands and wives can read together or separately if they would like.

It was early August, just a couple weeks before our youngest was heading off to his freshman year of college. Mark and I were calendaring for the fall, making sure he had my speaking engagements on his calendar, and I had his important business events on mine. We were also carving out a plan for seeing extended family and our grown kids.

I had ten solid days of speaking scheduled for the end of September. I was speaking at a church in Pennsylvania, then doing some television interviews in Toronto, then speaking in

Michigan, and finally, Indiana. We were talking through the logistics of that trip for me when all of a sudden it struck me. "Oh my goodness, Mark. You could go with me on this trip!"

"What are you talking about?" he responded. I continued, "We don't have any kids at home anymore so you don't have to stay back to manage the home front. Instead of me flying to all these places by myself, we could drive together! We could turn this into a road trip for you and me!"

Mark sat there for a minute taking in that idea. "I could, couldn't I?" he finally said. "I could take some time off and go with you. Won't you be near Niagara Falls? We've never been there before. We could do a night or two there!"

This was the first time we had considered how things might change for us as a couple in our encore years. Mark did decide to go with me on that trip, so we drove to Pennsylvania where I spoke. We then made our way to Niagara Falls to stay a couple of nights there, added some fun stops on our drive to Toronto for my interviews, stayed in a beautiful little cottage in Michigan where I spoke again before working our way to Indiana for three more speaking engagements and eventually back home to Illinois. It was a lot of driving, but also a lot of talking, exploring, and time for just the two of us. We loved it.

You've worked hard for your freedom. Now it's time to enjoy it individually, and if you're married, as a couple. Maybe you're like we were, and the lightbulb is just going on to the possibilities before you. Maybe you've already been empty-nesters for a while and you've been enjoying this later life honeymoon. It's also entirely possible you're not exactly experiencing the "full life" as it relates to marriage.

Unless you're in a second marriage, you've likely been together twenty years or more. You've also had this distraction called kids in front of you. This has kept you busy but not necessarily emotionally connected.

Regardless of where you sit on the marriage spectrum—madly in love and so glad for it to be just the two of you, or feeling disconnected and not sure what to do with your lackluster relationship—this is one part of your life where you need to see the possibilities of "something new bursting out" that we read about in Isaiah 43 (MSG). It's time to refresh, revive, or even restore what you have.

Mind the Gap

Several years ago, I had the opportunity to travel to London, England. I used the Underground (subway) for all my transportation. Every time I would get on or off the Underground, a voice would come on and say, "Mind the gap. Mind the gap." It was the English way of saying, "Watch your step. Be careful about the gap between the train and the train station podium you're exiting to or from."

I've thought about that phrase many times and how we can use that in other parts of our lives. Marriage is one of those places where we can have a "gap" we need to pay attention to. Maybe it's a communication gap, a sex gap, a connecting emotionally gap, or a having fun gap. It's unlikely you've made it through twenty or more years of raising kids without experiencing some kind of gap in your relationship. It's also entirely possible you need to mind a lot of gaps in your marriage because you've lost that lovin' feeling and you're not sure you can get it back.

Let me be the first to tell you that you can close the gaps in your marriage, even if those gaps are huge. You can breathe fresh life into a lifeless relationship. We're going to explore some of the common places where couples feel distance or disconnection in the empty nest years and some practical ways you can turn that around. Before we do that, however, let's lay the foundation for healthy marriages. Shoring the foundation gives us the footing we need to build on.

When I'm a Better ME, We're a Better WE

As couples we both bring dysfunction to the relationship. It doesn't matter if we've been married two years or forty-two years, we both still bring "junk in the trunk." Some of this comes from our family of origin, some of it comes from our own struggles with sin, some of it from our insecurity or pride, and some could come from previous relationships (previous dating relationships or a previous marriage if this isn't your first).

What's your junk? What are you bringing to the marriage table that is not healthy? Not sure? Here are a few questions that will help you identify some "junk" that isn't helping your marriage. If you're ready to dig into more self-reflection, check out the appendix for even more questions that will help you evaluate your contributions to your marriage.

Am I overly critical, causing my spouse to feel like he or she can't do anything right?

Do I have trouble finding my voice and sharing my thoughts and feelings?

Am I a "buck-up" person emotionally, disregarding my feelings and probably the feelings of others?

Is my tone of voice disrespectful in any way?

Have I been child-centered up to this point in my life?

Do I struggle with unrealistic expectations that keep me disappointed and discontent?

Do I always have to have my own way?

Is there something I need to forgive but I'm still holding onto?

Am I safe for my spouse to be honest with?

Can I ask for what I need or do I just get angry when my spouse doesn't do what I think he or she should?

Self-awareness is the first step to maturity and growth. We can't change something if we can't see it or won't look at it. Every question above and in the appendix that you resonate with represents a growth opportunity for you as an individual. This is growth you *need* to pursue because I can guarantee that every question you resonate with above *is* negatively affecting your marriage in some way.

Mark and I have been coaching marriages for several years now, and every evaluating question listed is something we've helped people untangle in their relationship. Don't make the mistake of thinking that your hurts, habits, and hang-ups[14] aren't affecting the people around you. Start doing the emotional, spiritual, and relational work to reduce the junk you're bringing to the table.

Begin with prayer, asking God to help you see the places you need growth. Ask Him for direction for next steps. Ask Him to help you connect the dots to the right people who can help you. Consider coaching or professional Christian counseling when you have a lot to untangle or when you're just ready to find the freedom you long for. You might even copy the questions in the appendix, highlighting the ones you need to do something about. If you walk into a counseling or coaching session knowing at least some of the issues you need to tackle, you'll be able to jump right in and get after it! It will still require work on your part to tackle lies, identify toxic thinking, and learn new ways of responding, but you'll move there faster for sure!

Now that we've considered the foundation, let's take a look at some of those places where we need to "mind the gap" in our marriage.

The communication gap

Dealing with kids keeps you talking about calendars, schedules, and the everyday stuff of life. It might have kept you talking about parenting strategies if you were trying to figure out how to best lead your young adult or even disagreeing if you both felt differently about what to do. For most couples, though, it's been a while since we talked about things we're interested in, or our hopes, dreams, and even struggles.

Most couples have communication ruts in their relationship. They're so used to interacting in certain ways even if those ways aren't healthy or helpful. One of the things we have to realize is that to make change happen we have to push through awkward to get to a new normal. So as we become accustomed to the new dynamics of no interruptions and no distractions, we may feel like we're not quite sure what to do with ourselves. Conversation may even feel forced. That's okay. Push through it to pave new communication roads. Here are a few questions to toss around:

How can I pray for you?

What's one thing that's weighing heavy on your heart?

Is there anything you're worrying about that would be helpful for me to know?

Now that it's just the two of us, what does a perfect evening look like for you?

Is there something we could do now together that we haven't in the past?

Is there a project that needs to be done that we could work on together?

Is there something you would love to do personally that we could make happen?

How are you doing with this empty nest transition? (Then listen and ask questions.)

Are there any new habits or traditions we need to create to see our kids/grandkids/parents on a regular basis?

If there's one thing you could do more of, what would it be?

Make sure you are safe for your spouse to communicate with. If you're quick to tell them why their ideas are not good ideas, you're not safe. If you are a realist and quick to tell them why their dream is unrealistic, you're not safe. If you're highly critical when you do any activity, you're not safe. Safe people are also good listeners. They listen to understand, not to disagree or insert their own opinions. Reflecting back what your spouse says is a good way to become a better listener. "What I hear you saying is . . ." is a phrase that will help you do that. You may not agree with what they're saying, but now's not the time to voice that. Instead, let him or her know you've heard them, asking questions to understand more. Resist the urge to "fix it," too. You might even ask, "Do you want to try to solve this, or do you just want me to listen and understand?"

Pay attention to places where you unintentionally undermine your spouse. For instance, let's say you've decided to go out to dinner. You say to your spouse, "You pick the restaurant this time. I picked last time. We'll go wherever you want to go." Then he or she says, "Okay, let's do Mexican." Then you respond with, "No, not Mexican, because I don't want to be tempted by the chips and salsa." So he or she says, "Okay, Italian," and you respond with, "No, not Italian either, because I'll be tempted by the bread." So can your spouse really choose where to go eat, or can he or she only choose where to go eat if you approve? This is an unhealthy dynamic too many marriages experience. Don't undermine your spouse. Mind the communication gap by creating new ways of talking, listening, and responding.

The "having fun" gap

For most of us, when we were dating we were all about having fun together. We went to concerts, sporting events, and picnics. We went to the movies, hung out with other couples, and went mini-golfing.

Some of those things went away because we didn't have the funds once kids came along. We certainly didn't have the time in the same way we did when we were dating. For some of us, we became very child-centered and didn't want to leave the kids to take time for the marriage. So our twenty-five-year-old marriage may have forgotten how to have fun!

We certainly experienced that. It was seven years ago when we started riding a motorcycle together. Mark had restored a vintage Honda motorcycle and ridden for a few years, but I was fearful and not excited about riding at all. I finally decided to push through my fear and make it happen. We got Bluetooth helmets so we could talk to each other and started taking country rides on a regular basis. Believe it or not, I grew to love it—maybe even more than Mark does! Last summer Mark communicated that he wasn't comfortable riding anymore. "Too many distracted drivers out there. I don't want us to be someone's hood ornament," he said. I think I've missed it more than he has. He's currently restoring an MG Midget right now. He says that's our new motorcycle.

One couple we know has discovered their favorite date nights are taking painting classes. Neither one had painted before, but they gave it a try one night and found they both loved it. Now they're hooked! You might try your local library or community college for continuing or one-time offerings and events.

Mark and I recently started "adventure dining" on Thursday nights. Every Thursday night we go out to dinner somewhere we've never been to before. This has been a fun way to explore new tastes, experiences, and even cultures. We're moving away from the major chain restaurants to more unique, smaller, only-in-our-town establishments. It's added a unique twist to our date night.

Another new habit we've begun is making dinner together. For most of our married life, I was in charge of dinner and carried that responsibility on my own. Now that it's just the two of us, Mark has started helping me with the chopping, preparing, and cooking. We share about our day as we work together. Creating new habits and doing things together you didn't before is healthy for your marriage.

My friend Donna and her husband have been working to develop new traditions for the two of them to do alone. Donna shared, "For our 25th wedding anniversary, we didn't have the money or time to go on an expensive vacation. I picked a surprise destination (usually within a two-hour drive) and we spent one night at a hotel for each month for the entire year (hot tub and fireplace included). My husband loved trying to guess where we were going as we were driving to each location. And we celebrated each month all year long! This year is our 35th, and I'm thinking maybe we will have to do this again!" What a great idea!

Sometimes "fun" might mean hanging out with other couples. Enjoying a couple's small group, or dinner out with another couple, or even taking a trip with friends may now be more of a possibility than in the past. Couple friends can be challenging to find, however, because sometimes the husbands click but the wives do not, or the wives click but the husbands don't. If you yearn for couple friendships, keep pursuing possibilities. Don't give up. Keep asking God to connect the dots to just the right friendship.

> **Couples who find themselves at home alone together after the kids are gone sometimes forget the importance of still dating and having fun together.**

Couples who find themselves at home alone together after the kids are gone sometimes forget the importance of still dating and having fun together. If you had a regular date night while you were raising your kids—good for you. Now keep it! If you got out of the habit of dating when you were raising your family, it's time to return to it. Set aside one night a week (you don't have to hire a sitter—so yes, one night a week!), and start having fun together again!

The connecting emotionally gap

I was emotionally constipated for twenty-seven years of our marriage. I know that seems like a funny thing to say, but it's the truth. In many marriages, it's the man who's emotionally shut down, but there are plenty of women like me who are as well.

I was raised in a loving home by loving parents, but when it came to the hard stuff of life, we were strong. We bucked up. I had no idea how years of that caused me to disregard emotions in myself and others, but it did. Add in my type-A-driven, logical, firstborn, thinker personality and temperament and I didn't have much use for vulnerable feelings. I was strong. Cried only in private. And was quick to tell others why they should be that way too. I had no idea that my lack of emotional connection and strong exterior was sending an unintentional message to my husband that I didn't need him.

As I shared earlier in the book, it was a marriage counselor who first said to me, "Jill, when did you start believing the lie that feelings don't matter?" "I'm not so sure that's a lie," I replied. "Yes, it is. You are created in the image of God and God is a feeling God. He has emotions. So feelings *do* matter," he said. That conversation gave me quite a bit to chew on. I started asking God to show me where that lie was planted, and He began to bring memories to my mind. I started to see things through a different lens.

Connecting with my emotional side has made me a much more compassionate wife, mom, and nana. I'm a better friend because of it. A better leader, too. I've also closed the gap I was causing in our marriage—the emotionally connected gap. I can now share my struggles with Mark. I can let him comfort me when I'm sad. Heck, I can admit when I'm sad!

When we struggle with emotional connection, we often make love with our eyes closed. Closing that gap, we become comfortable with eye contact, even in the most intimate moments of life. We're more sensitive to what's going on with others. We even increase our ability to read body language, sensing when someone is struggling with something they haven't quite yet found the words to communicate.

If you avoid emotion, get intentional about closing this gap. Set up a session with a Christian counselor or a marriage coach. You're missing out on the beautiful gift of intimacy in marriage. IN-TO-ME-SEE that is. Your connection with God, with your spouse, and your kids will deepen in a way you can't even imagine.

The sex gap

By the time the kids are leaving home and just when you have the freedom to chase each other around the house naked, that's when aging starts to play some ugly tricks on us. Most empty nest couples experience some kind of gap they need to be "minding" as it relates to sexual intimacy.

It seems unfair that men have the height of their sexual

drive in their twenties and thirties (when testosterone levels are the highest) while women seem to come alive sexually in their forties and fifties (often because the possibility of pregnancy is removed from the picture and kids aren't wearing them out as much). At the same time, menopause and aging start to change things in the bedroom. Add to that side effects from medication, illness, or depression and the sex gap becomes even wider. Too many couples just let sex go rather than being intentional about addressing the issues they're having.

If the gap is being caused by physical issues, the first step to closing the gap is a chat with your doctor. Too many couples suffer in silence when there are ways to treat the challenges they are experiencing. Yes, I know, it's uncomfortable to talk about that stuff with a doctor. For the sake of your marriage, however, you must! Vaginal dryness can be a challenge for some perimenopausal or menopausal women. While you may never have needed to use a lubricant before, you might need to add it to your bedside table in this encore season of life. Some men begin to struggle with impotence. Again, a chat with the doctor can begin the process of turning that around.

If the gap is being caused by emotional issues, an appointment with a counselor is a good place to start. Maybe you've been carrying emotional "junk in the trunk" as it relates to sex for most of your marriage. Now you have the ability to focus on yourself and find the freedom you've always longed for.

When it comes to sex, we need to become adaptable in our empty nest years. Couples report sex both increasing and decreasing after kids leave the home. It's likely that you and your spouse still have differing drives in some way or another, so meeting in the middle is important. Perhaps you'll adapt to a different frequency, or you may get creative and enjoy each other in different ways physically than you had before, but never give up on the physical intimacy aspect of your marriage.[15]

What does the Bible say about sex as it relates to expanding our view of sexual intimacy? Proverbs 5:15 tells us to "drink water from your own cistern, running water from your own well." This is an allegory from Solomon, urging us to be pure in our married life. We need to keep our eyes, hands, and heart on only our spouse.

Then there's Song of Solomon. Song of Solomon is a delightfully sensual poem written about a love relationship between a husband and wife. I like to say it's God's book on sex. Dr. Juli Slattery, founder of Authentic Intimacy, says, "People are often surprised at this special book in the Bible because it's quite erotic and uses code words to describe the physical relationship in marriage. The 'fruit' mentioned in Song of Solomon refers to the male genitalia and the garden refers to the female genitalia. There are aphrodisiacs mentioned including milk and honey as it relates to enjoying each other."[16] Understanding that context, chapter 2 verse 3 says, "Like an apple tree among the trees of the forest is my beloved among the young men. I delight to sit in his shade, and his fruit is sweet to my taste." In chapter 4 verse 16 the young woman continues, "Awake, north wind, and come, south wind! Blow on my garden, that its fragrance may spread everywhere. Let my beloved come into his garden and taste its choice fruits."

God has given sex to us in marriage to experience the closest intimate relationship we can have with another person. It's designed for a married couple to have a private playground for two. If you're experiencing a sexual intimacy gap, don't let it continue to widen. Take the next right step to close that gap today.

No More Perfect Marriages

Our marriage has been through the wringer. In fact, eight years ago it went off the tracks. Mark decided to leave pastoring after twenty years in church ministry. He underestimated how much of his identity had been tied up in being a pastor. Over the next year he spiraled into a full-on midlife crisis, affair included. He eventually left me, determined to ride off into the sunset in this new relationship. It was the darkest year of my life.

I did not feel like God was releasing me from our marriage. I stood for it. Believed in it. Even had compassion for my husband who had lost his way. Don't get me wrong, I cried more tears in that year than I probably have in my lifetime. I was hurt, rejected, and heartbroken. Yet I still believed in us.

It was Easter Sunday 2012 when my husband had his own personal resurrection. The blinders came off. He made a U-turn, fully surrendering to God. It was the end of a yearlong fight for our relationship but the beginning of a two-year cleanup. We had gaps after gaps after gaps. Not only that, but some of the gaps were miles in size.

That distance wasn't only caused by my husband's unfaithfulness. I had to look at what I brought to the party. I had to own some of those evaluating questions in the appendix. Mark and I did the hard work to close our gaps . . . even the "I don't love you anymore" gap. Yep, we both felt that and I'm telling you from someone who has been there, even that gap can be closed.

Mark and Jill 1.0 existed while we were raising our kids. It had its strengths and its weaknesses. Mark and Jill 2.0 is what we're experiencing after our crisis and in the empty nest years. We love the new us. It was hard work to get there, but worth every effort we made, every penny we spent, and every hard place we pushed through. We eventually wrote about that journey in *No More Perfect Marriages*. It's a book that's helping good marriages become great and hurting marriages find hope and help. We also established www.NoMorePerfectMarriages.com as a gathering point for all our marriage resources. Check it out—there's something there for you!

The empty nest years give you the possibility of a 2.0 experience. If things are good, you can keep growing and learning together in order to keep gaps from forming. If things are hard, you can change that as well. Even if you're the only one who chooses to change, your marriage will change. If both of you are willing to tackle the gaps, no matter what they are and how big they are, God is all about doing something "brand-new" in this new season of life!

Truth for Today:

"Love is patient and kind; love does not envy or boast; it is not arrogant or rude. It does not insist on its own way; it is not irritable or resentful; it does not rejoice at wrong-doing, but rejoices with the truth. Love bears all things, believes all things, hopes all things, endures all things."

1 Corinthians 13:4–7 (ESV)

Take the Next Step:

Text your spouse a flirty text right now before you forget! (Need help with ideas of what to text? Check out https://www.jillsavage.org/flirt-alert/ for ideas!)

Talk with God:

Lord, help me see my spouse through Your eyes. Help me respond with love, compassion, forgiveness, and grace when I bump into their imperfect. I admit that I've contributed to some gaps in our marriage. I have some "junk in my trunk" that I need to dig into. Give me the wisdom and courage to own what's mine and pursue my own emotional health. In Jesus' name, amen.

Chapter 11

GRAB HOLD
OF GOD'S HAND

"**I dreaded returning** to that now empty house. But as I entered the front door and looked down the length of the hall and up the steps leading to the children's now vacant rooms, suddenly it wasn't empty. I was greeted by a living Presence, and I realized anew how true His last words were: 'Lo, I am with you'" (Matt. 28:20).[17] I could so relate to those words that were shared by Ruth Graham, wife of Billy Graham, mother of five, as she processed the emotions of her empty nest.

As our kids leave, it's even more important for us to grab hold of God's hand. His unchanging presence in our heart and our home is what we need to bring stability to our ever-changing circumstances. Jesus understands change. He knows disappointment. He gets grief. You and I have to grab hold of the hand of the Friend who understands.

Just Say Yes

When God put Adam and Eve in the garden of Eden, He had a perfect personal relationship with them. The Creator and the created were connected. God gave them only one rule (not to eat of the Tree of the Knowledge of Good and Evil), and when they broke that rule, their relationship with God was broken. With that one wrong choice, sin entered into this world. That sin now separated the Creator from the created. You can read about this in the first book of the Bible, Genesis, chapters 1 through 3.

The Old Testament is the first part of the Bible. It is God's story before Jesus lived on this earth. Throughout the Old Testament, we see God's efforts to restore relationship with humankind through an established law and required sacrifices, such as grain and animals. Animal sacrifice foreshadowed, or helped people look ahead to, the sacrifice of Jesus.[18] Animal sacrifices were important because "without the shedding of blood there is no forgiveness" (Heb. 9:22). But no sacrifice could once and for all cover a person's sin so he or she could have a restored relationship with a holy God. Sacrifices had to be made over and over. Until Jesus.

In the New Testament, we see how God, out of His incredible love for us, sent His Son, Jesus, to this earth to be the final, perfect sacrifice. John 3:16 (NLT) tells us this: "This is how God loved the world: He gave his one and only Son, so that everyone who believes in him will not perish but have eternal life." God sent His Son to this earth, in part to be a living demonstration of how to live, but most importantly, to live a sinless life and then die on a cross in our place. His life was exchanged for ours. That is why Jesus is called our Redeemer. However, God will never force Himself on us. He wants a personal relationship with us, where we interact with Him on a regular basis.

This is not about going to church. Church attendance isn't what puts us in relationship with God. Billy Sunday humorously once said, "Going to church doesn't make you a Christian any more than going to a garage makes you an automobile." Being part of a church family is something we do to stay connected to God and to stay connected to other believers. It's important; however, it's not what establishes us in a personal relationship with God.

You see, God reaches out His hand, inviting us to grab it and say yes to Him. You can do that in church on a Sunday morning, or you can do that sitting here with this book in your hands. God wants a friendship with *you*. Jesus exchanged His perfect life for our imperfect lives. He saved us from a life and from an eternity spent apart from God. That's why He is called our Savior.

If you have never said yes to God, you can do that now by praying these words or something similar: *God, I want to know You. I want my identity to be determined by You and only You. Thank You for sending Jesus to this earth. I accept Him as my Savior, and I want Him to be the leader of my life. Today I'm grabbing Your hand that's reaching out to me. In Jesus' name, amen.*

If you prayed that prayer for the very first time, I want you to email me and tell me! (You'll find my email at the back of the book.) Just put "I said Yes!" in the subject line so I'll make sure to see it and celebrate with you! If you said yes to God a while ago, let this be your reminder of the beautiful exchange God made for you.

God's in the redemption business, but not just once in our lives. God continues to redeem. That means He forgives the past and gives us a future. The Bible tells us He says He will exchange beauty for ashes (Isa. 61:3). This means God can make something beautiful out of the broken places in our lives.

One of my favorite verses in the Bible is Joel 2:25, where God says He will redeem what the locusts have eaten. This means He will restore our lives after devastation. We don't have to worry about plagues of locusts in this day and age, but there are other "plagues" that cause damage in our lives. Maybe you're plagued with worry over a wayward child. Plagued with resentment over a broken relationship. Have you been plagued with guilt when you did something you shouldn't have done or said something you shouldn't have said? Have you been plagued with pain after someone you love has betrayed your trust? God longs to redeem those hurt places. He wants to exchange them for something new. He wants to restore and renew the broken places in our lives.

We need God's power in our life in order to both let go and grab hold of what we need to in these transitional years. We can't do it in our own power, but we can do it when we're partnered with Him! He loves us more than we can imagine and understands more than we could ever comprehend.

The Friend Who Understands

When Jesus lived on this earth, He was fully God but also fully man. That means He experienced every human emotion we experience. I love how Hebrews 4:14–16 reads in *The Message*: "Now that we know what we have—Jesus, this great High Priest with ready access to God—let's not let it slip through our fingers. We don't have a priest who is out of touch with our reality. He's been through weakness and testing, experienced it all—all but the sin. So let's walk right up to him and get what he is so ready to give. Take the mercy, accept the help." So because Jesus was fully God *and* fully man, He gets us. He understands life. And thanks to His sacrifice on the cross, no rules, no further sacrifices are necessary for us to approach God; Jesus is the only mediator (1 Tim. 2:5).

Jesus knows change. He often traveled from town to town teaching others about God. We're reminded of this in Matthew 8:20 when Jesus said, "Foxes have dens and birds have nests, but the Son of Man has no place to lay his head."

Jesus knows disappointment. When he was in the garden of Gethsemane, He asked his friends to keep watch as He went off to pray by Himself. When He returned to His friends, He found that they had fallen asleep. They let Him down (Matt. 26:36–46).

Jesus knows betrayal. Jesus' friend Judas sold Him out for thirty pieces of silver (Matt. 26:15). Peter denied he knew Him on three different occasions (John 18:15–27). Jesus understands broken trust.

Jesus knows physical exhaustion. John 4:6 tells us that Jesus was tired from his journey. Matthew 8:23–27 tells of how Jesus and His disciples were in a boat when a great storm came up— but He was so tired He would have slept through it if the disciples hadn't awakened Him. He knows what it feels like to hardly be able to keep your eyes open!

Jesus knows loss. When His friend Lazarus died, Jesus wept (John 11:35). He shed tears in His pain, letting us know that it's okay to cry when we experience loss. Jesus didn't only lose His good friend Lazarus, He also lost His dear friend and cousin, John the Baptist. John went ahead of Jesus' public ministry and prepared the way for Him. John was, however, arrested by Herod and executed. When John's disciples tell Jesus that John has died, Jesus gets in a boat and heads to a desolate place (Matt. 14:13). Jesus was grieving. He was heartbroken and needed to spend some time thinking and praying. Jesus knows the human pain of loss. In those moments where you find yourself grieving this transition in life, talk to your God. He gets it.

> When you and I grab hold of God's hand, we are grabbing a lifeline. We're throwing down an anchor that keeps us from being shipwrecked in the storms of life.

When you and I grab hold of God's hand, we are grabbing a lifeline. We're throwing down an anchor that keeps us from being shipwrecked in the storms of life. Hebrews 6:19 (ESV) reminds us of this truth—"We have this as a sure and steadfast anchor of the soul." You and I need this anchor during the emotionally disorienting empty nest transition. He's the one thing that does not change in our life.

Our Marching Orders

When Jesus is our leader, we get our marching orders from Him. That happens through the Bible, through prayer, through the nudges of the Holy Spirit, and often from the counsel of others who follow Him. The one thing He asks us to do is to "steward" or manage well the life He's given us. As we launch into a new season of life, it a good time for us to consider how we're doing stewarding what God's given us. Let's explore some parts of our life we need to be managing well.

Steward your time

"Look carefully then how you walk, not as unwise but as wise." Ephesians 5:15 (ESV)

Every one of us has 168 hours in our week. How we use those hours is completely up to us. Have you ever considered, however, that you are actually a steward of the hours God has given you? You are a caretaker, a guardian, an overseer, a manager of your time. Are you using it well?

When we look at the life of Christ, one of the first things we notice is that He is intentional about spending time with God. There are many verses that tell us that Jesus pulled away from the crowd to pray. As we think about stewarding our time, we can start by following Jesus' lead. Find a time in your day to read God's Word and talk with Him. That may be morning, afternoon, or evening—whatever works best for you. It might even be throughout the day.

I recently read a biography of Ruth and Billy Graham, and one of the habits Ruth had in her life was to leave her Bible open wherever she was working. If she was ironing, the Bible was open on the ironing board. If she was cooking, her Bible was open on the kitchen counter. She would just "snack" on God's Word all day. Reading about her habit challenged me to think differently about time I could have with God!

We can certainly talk to God all day. As we put on our make-up. As we drive. As we cook. We can even listen to the Bible these days through the Bible app on our smartphone as we're doing those same things. As we spend time with God, we get our marching orders and He helps us to be a good steward of our time!

Steward your physical health

"Do you not know that your body is a temple of the Holy Spirit within you, whom you have from God? You are not your own, for you were

bought with a price. So glorify God in your body." 1 Corinthians 6:19–20 (ESV)

It was the call no one wants to receive. "Mrs. Savage, we have the results from your breast biopsy. It is showing cancer. We need to get you connected to a surgeon today." A few weeks earlier I'd had my annual mammogram. I'd been called back for a follow-up sonogram or additional mammogram pictures in the past, but never called back for a biopsy. All those other call-backs revealed nothing, so I wasn't particularly worried about the biopsy either. Needless to say, my world turned upside down that day.

I was diagnosed with Stage 1 Triple Negative breast cancer. Most breast cancers are fueled by either estrogen, progesterone, or something called HER2. Triple-negative breast cancer is negative for all three of those fuels, meaning they don't know what is fueling this cancer, so they throw everything at it: surgery, chemotherapy, and radiation. It was a long seven months of treatment. I lost a portion of my breast and all of my hair, including a significant part of my eyebrows and eyelashes that have still never returned.

What I learned on my breast cancer journey is that early detection saves lives. I was a stage 1 diagnosis because we caught it early. You and I have to steward this body God has given us. Take care of it. Keep it healthy. Catch things early. What screenings are you overdue for? Are you keeping up with your annual gynecological appointment? What about your annual mammogram? If you're at least fifty, have you had your first colonoscopy? Are you going to your dentist regularly? When was the last time you had a physical?

If you need to make any of those appointments or others you might be aware of, set this book down and make the appointment—today. Do it for yourself *and* for your family. They'd like for you to be around for a while!

When it comes to stewarding our body, in addition to screenings, we need to water it, feed it, rest it, and move it. Are you intentionally drinking half your body weight in ounces of water each day? I slice up oranges and freeze them, then throw a slice or two in my water each day. This helps me enjoy the taste better and keeps me drinking my water all day.

Having cancer changed how I "feed" my body. Far less sugar, far more whole foods, little to no processed foods, and we eat out less often because we can eat healthier at home. Are you at a healthy BMI (Body Mass Index)? Is there a next right step you can take in feeding your body well?

One of the best parts of the empty nest season of life is you're likely not sleep deprived anymore. No more waiting up for a teenager to come home, no more middle of the night feedings, no more trying to get hundreds of things done after the kids go to bed. If your body is left to wake on its own, how many hours of sleep does it require? Whatever that is, shoot for it. Resting our body builds our immune system and reduces stress.

When I finished my cancer treatment my oncologist told me I had three jobs to do to help prevent a recurrence:

(1) Eat nutritionally.

(2) Stay at a healthy weight and BMI.

(3) Exercise daily.

I've done well with the first two, but I'm still trying to find that right rhythm for number three. We need to be moving our body. This keeps us flexible and strong. It also builds immunity. I've already mentioned the early morning kickboxing class. What are you doing to move this body God has given you? What's a next right step in exercise?

Steward your money

"Honor the Lord with your wealth and with the firstfruits of all your produce." Proverbs 3:9 (ESV)

When it was first just Mark and me at home, I consistently made too much food at every meal. I'd been used to cooking for seven for so long that I wasn't quite sure how to cook for two. Sure, we'd be gradually paring down the number of people around the table, but old habits die hard! There are two places, however, that I had no trouble adjusting: money and laundry. I appreciate that, for the most part, we only have to split our money two ways instead of seven, and I'm happy to have to do laundry only once a week and call it done.

Money was a little complicated for us because one year before we became empty-nesters, I left my job leading Hearts at Home and we took a huge hit in the income department.

We're still working to make our entrepreneur journey turn into full-time income for both of us. However, when we were raising our kids sometimes there was more month than money. With not needing to split the income into so many pieces, even with a reduced income we've noticed a welcome difference.

When we're raising kids, most of us are in bit of a survival mode. If you're married, only one of you is likely managing the money side of things. If that's you, it's probably time to give your spouse a tour of the bills, processes, investments, passwords, and such. If your spouse has been the one managing the money, it's probably time to request a financial tour. Pulling together a "financial notebook" where those things can be found is also wise. I created one several years ago, and Mark and our adult kids know where it is should there ever be a reason they would need it.

Now's the time to review emergency funds and long-term savings. Do you have enough cash in the bank to fix your car or replace an appliance that quits working? Do you have three months of living expenses tucked away in case something were to happen to your job or your spouse's job? Is there any debt you need to be tackling aggressively?

The empty nest is a perfect time to review retirement and how you're doing funding it. Set up an appointment with a financial planner to evaluate where you are in your retirement goals and to discuss any ways you might want to adjust your strategies.

Don't forget to review giving commitments. Are you tithing to your church? If you are, do you want to increase your giving in any way? Is there something you believe in that you'd like to support in addition?

Ask God to show you what you need to see as it relates to your money and your giving. He's the one who's trusted you with what He's giving you. He'll most definitely show you the way!

You're Not Alone

You're designed to walk through life holding the hand of God. He's got the big picture in mind, and you can trust Him to lead and guide you along the way. He also gave you an important instruction book, the Bible, that will guide you to be a good steward of all that He's given you.

We live in a broken world. Walking with God won't keep us from experiencing the broken parts of life on earth, but it will assure us we won't walk through them alone or without guidance. Sometimes we're affected by the ripples of other people's brokenness. When that happens, Jesus understands. He's walked more than a mile in our shoes.

In this encore, you have a new opportunity to make the most of the life God has given you. There are things that need to be let go of and things you need to grab hold of. Grabbing hold of God will give you the strength and show you how to do both of those . . . sometimes even at the same time!

Truth for Today:

"Now that we know what we have—Jesus, this great
High Priest with ready access to God—let's not let it
slip through our fingers. We don't have a priest who is
out of touch with our reality. He's been through weakness
and testing, experienced it all—all but the sin. So
let's walk right up to him and get what he is so ready
to give. Take the mercy, accept the help."

Hebrews 4:14–16 (MSG)

Take the Next Step:

Pull out your Bible to the book of Proverbs. Read whatever chapter in Proverbs matches the day of the month
it is today. Do the same tomorrow. Keep reading
Proverbs daily to get your daily dose of wisdom.

Talk with God:

*Lord, thank You for the hope we have in You. I'm grateful
for Jesus showing us the way. Help me keep my eyes on You.
So often I'm distracted by the mountain when I need to
be looking at You, the Mountain Mover. I know You're
holding me, leading me, and loving me, so help me sense
Your presence each day. In Jesus' name, amen.*

Chapter 12

YOUR ENCORE

I love the theater and I especially love musicals. I caught the performing bug in high school and it influenced my decision to pursue a degree in choral music education. I've had my favorite roles over the years including Hodel in *Fiddler on the Roof* and Minnie Fay in *Hello, Dolly!* I've also served as the musical director for a community theater performance and emceed our church's Living Christmas Tree program for several years. No matter the show, no matter the setting, my absolute favorite part of every musical performance is the encore.

Why? you might ask. Because people think the show is over when it really isn't. There's still more to come. It's a fun little surprise that delivers extra music to folks who aren't ready to be done. Do you see why I consider the empty nest season of life an encore? We may think the show is over, but it really isn't. Surprise—there's so much more to come!

I also love the encore because of the applause. This is when the hard work of the show is rewarded. In motherhood, our applause is found in the sense of accomplishment we feel. It's found in the freedom we experience from the daily responsibilities of motherhood. It may or may not be expressed by our kids. If it is, it will likely be after they become parents themselves. Most importantly though, it is the applause you need to know is coming from your audience of One. God knows you worked hard. He saw every sacrifice you made to get this child from birth to launch. He's seen your personal growth in the journey and He's saying, "Good job. Now let's work together in these next years you have!"

Your Reprise

In musical theater, a reprise is the repeating of an earlier song. Often used in an encore, a musical reprise allows the cast to go back and sing portions of some of the songs in the show. They don't usually sing any song fully, but rather a compilation of the best parts of each song.

This is your reprise. You still get to sing some of the songs you loved singing like nurturing, encouraging, cheering on, mentoring, teaching, loving, and listening. Sometimes you'll get to sing those for your adult kids, grandkids (if and when they arrive), and sometimes you'll get to reprise those songs with others that God sends your way. The beautiful thing is that you get to sing the best parts of those songs without having to sing all the "verses" like being up all night with a crying baby, or trying to figure out why the toddler is fussy, or managing homework, or paying for clothes, shoes, and school supplies, or worrying about them driving by themselves for the first time. You can, in essence, play to your strengths.

For instance, I love helping a child learn to read. It's satisfying to coach them to sound out the letters and then seeing the lightbulb come on when they figure out the word. I still get to do that in small doses with my grandkids. I enjoy cooking for my family—it's how I say "I love you!" I still get to cook for my kids on occasion, but I'm no longer responsible for feeding them every single night. I can snuggle babies in the church nursery, but I don't have to be up all night with them! I still get to do many of the things I love, but in smaller, more manageable portions. This gives me the time and energy for my full encore.

The Next Stage

Your reprise consists of bits and pieces of things you've done before that you get to do again, but in smaller portions. It will be part of your encore but not the whole thing. Have you ever been to a concert where a musical artist or a band performs and you get to the end of the show and realize, "Wait. They never sang _____." Then all of a sudden the lights come on, the music starts again, and it's that song! This is the song they're known for. It's like this is the song they were created to do. The concert was great and the music was solid but the encore is what you came for.

I imagine that's sort of how God views us in our empty nest years. Our concert—the years we spent raising our kids—was solid. There was some great music played and there were some songs we absolutely loved. We became stronger, more experienced, and more knowledgeable in those years. We thought the show was over, except it wasn't. The lights kicked on and the music started again. This time we not only got to do a reprise, but we get the opportunity to possibly perform a new song. The one we were made to sing. The one we put on the back burner to raise our family or the new one we're writing right now. This is where we get to leverage all we learned and offer it to the world in a fresh, new way. New mission fields. Rediscovered passions. New or refreshed friendships. A revived marriage. A new or revitalized relationship with God.

There Is a Season

We started in Ecclesiastes. As we bring our time together to an end, let's expand our picture a bit and look at the context of our verse. This is Ecclesiastes 3:1–8 from *The Message*:

There's an opportune time to do things, a right time for everything on the earth:

A right time for birth and another for death,
A right time to plant and another to reap,
A right time to kill and another to heal,
A right time to destroy and another to construct,

A right time to cry and another to laugh,
A right time to lament and another to cheer,
A right time to make love and another to abstain,
A right time to embrace and another to part,
A right time to search and another to count your losses,
A right time to hold on and another to let go,
A right time to rip out and another to mend,
A right time to shut up and another to speak up,
A right time to love and another to hate,
A right time to wage war and another to make peace.

We've talked about so many of these "right times" on the pages we've spent together. Our focus was primarily on holding on and letting go, but so many of these affirm our lessons learned and wisdom shared for navigating this unique time in our life. There are right times and right responses. May we be intentional about embracing both of those.

Yes, we need to let go. We need to let go of expectations, guilt, opinions, traditions, our child's problems, and the misplaced worship of idols of the heart. With our hands open, we are now in a position to hold on to our new mission fields, passions, friendships, marriage for those who are, and most importantly, God's hand. When we make this letting-go-and-holding-on exchange, this is when we move from empty to full. There may be an empty nest, but there's a full life to be experienced.

God has plans for you. Plans to give you a hope and a future.

He wants you to be alert and to be fully present because He's doing something brand-new!

The curtain has risen, the music has started once again. What song are you singing for your encore? What reprise are you enjoying? Whatever it is, enjoy it to the fullest. Oh, and don't miss the applause. Your audience of One is whispering, "Well done. Now let's get going on what I have next for you."

APPENDIX: JUNK IN THE TRUNK

What's your junk in the trunk? What are you bringing to the marriage table that is not healthy? Not sure? Here are some questions that will help you identify some "junk" that isn't helping your marriage. Underline, circle, or write down in a journal the ones you resonate with (or your spouse has mentioned to you):

Am I overly critical, causing my spouse to feel like he or she can't do anything right?

Do I have trouble finding my voice and sharing my thoughts and feelings?

Am I a "buck-up" person emotionally disregarding my feelings and probably the feelings of others?

Do I struggle with anger?

Am I more committed to my family of origin than to my marriage?

Am I dismissive of my partner's feelings or concerns?

Am I controlling of him or her?

Is my tone of voice disrespectful in any way?

Have I been child-centered up to this point in my life?

Have I resisted asking for help with my marriage or other parts of my life?

Do I struggle with unrealistic expectations that keep me disappointed and discontent?

Am I naïve and not protecting my marriage by spending time with someone of the opposite sex who is not my spouse?

Do I always have to be right?

Do I have trouble apologizing?

Are my actions loving?

Are my words loving?

Do I tell my spouse daily that I love him or her?

Do I know my spouse's love language? If so, do I speak it? (If you're not sure, visit 5lovelanguages.com.)

Do I send the message with my words and actions that I tolerate my spouse or cherish him or her? Do I always have to have my own way?

Am I selfish and most often think only of what I want to do?

Do I hint rather than ask directly for what I need?

Am I secretive? Am I keeping things from my spouse?

Do I keep my thoughts to myself and rarely let my spouse know when I'm thinking about something?

Do I expect my spouse to read my mind?

Is there something I need to forgive but I'm still holding on to?

Have I given my spouse reason to mistrust me?

Do I think anything my spouse does differently from me is wrong?

Do I think my way is the right way?

Do I talk so much that my spouse can't get a word in edgewise?

Do I listen to hear my spouse and understand him or her, or do I listen to argue?

Am I quick to blame someone else rather than own my own stuff?

Am I fearful and allowing my fears to keep me from doing things with my spouse?

Am I a workaholic and more committed to work than to my spouse?

Am I confusing "providing for" with "caring for" and "being emotionally connected to" my spouse?

Do I take things personally that aren't about me at all?

Do I struggle with wanting sex?

Am I looking at or watching pornography?

Am I believing that another relationship might be the answer?

Do I struggle physically with sex? Have I talked to a doctor about my issues?

Am I feeling hopeless in my marriage? In life?

Do I struggle feeling that God is for me?

Am I safe for my spouse to share his or her heart or struggles with me?

Do I respond steadily or react emotionally?

Am I safe for my spouse to give me feedback about what I bring negatively to the relationship?

Am I safe for my spouse to be honest with?

Can I ask for what I need, or do I just get angry when my spouse doesn't do what I think he or she should?

Could I be depressed? If so, have I seen a doctor to discuss that?

Do I rationalize why it's okay for me to mistreat my spouse?

Am I always trying to change my spouse?

Am I praying "God, change him," or "God, change her," more than "God, change me"?

Am I emotionally detached from my spouse?

Am I disconnected from God?

ACKNOWLEDGMENTS

The older I get the more I understand we're better together! This book is what it is because of these people:

Every mom who has shared her story, frustrations, joys, and discoveries with me. Your honesty has helped make the message of this book stronger.

My pre-readers who gave fabulous insight: Addie, Becky, Beth, Bonnie D., Bonnie M., Becky, Deb, Donna, Julie, Laury, Lorrie, Margie, Tammy, Tricia, and Trina. Thank you for reading, challenging, adding thoughts, asking questions, creating sticky statements, and making suggestions. You helped make this a better book!

My prayer team: Thank you for standing in the gap for me while I wrote. Special thanks to Becky who keeps my prayer team "in the know!"

The Moody Publishers team: I love partnering with you! You guys are the best!

Sandra Bishop at Transatlantic Literary Agency: I love creating books with you. Thank you for representing me well!

My kids Anne, Evan, Erica, Nicolai, and Austin: Thank you

for letting me share your stories. You help other families in so many ways!

Mark: I love doing this empty nest life with you! Mark and Jill 2.0 is the best!

God: Thank You for giving us the opportunity to be part of Your work here on earth. It's a pleasure to lead others to the full life You have designed!

NOTES

1. Claudia Wallis, "What Makes Teens Tick," *Time* (May 10, 2004).
2. Brenda Garrison, *Love No Matter What: When Your Kids Make Decisions You Don't Agree With* (Nashville: Thomas Nelson, 2013), 22.
3. https://www.stlouisfed.org/on-the-economy/2015/october/millennials-living-home-student-debt-housing-labor.
4. Claudia Wallis, "What Makes Teens Tick."
5. Marianne Burke, guest author, "Sharing the Family's Side of the Disease of Addiction," www.breakingthecyclescom/blog/2015/03/09/sharing-familys-side-disease-addiction.
6. Carol Kent, *When I Lay My Isaac Down: Unshakable Faith in Unthinkable Circumstances* (Colorado Springs: NavPress, 2004), 169–70.
7. Carolyn Daitch, quoted in Kate Bayless, "What Is Helicopter Parenting?," Parents, https://www.parents.com/parenting/better-parenting/what-is-helicopter-parenting/.
8. Ann Dunnewold, quoted in ibid. Ann Dunnewold, PhD, is a licensed psychologist and author of *Even June Cleaver Forgets the Juice Box* (Deerfield Beach, FL: Health Communications, Inc., 2007).
9. Christopher Yuan and Angela Yuan, *Out of a Far Country: A Gay Son's Journey to God. A Broken Mother's Search for Hope* (Colorado Springs: Water-Brook, 2011).
10. Paul Tripp, "The Idol of Control," PaulTripp.com, May 17, 2013, https://www.paultripp.com/articles/posts/the-idol-of-control.
11. Paul Tripp, "The Idol of Success," PaulTripp.com, May 3, 2013, https://www.paultripp.com/articles/posts/the-idol-of-success.
12. Ibid.
13. JAMSavage Ministries has an affiliate relationship with Compassion International. What that means is that, at no additional cost to you, we may receive compensation if you click through on this affiliate link. We only partner with ministries we use and love ourselves! If you use this link to sponsor a child, thank you for bringing hope to that child and helping to support our ministry to families! www.compassion.com/emptynest.

14. Hurts, habits, and hang-ups phrase is used by Celebrate Recovery, www
.celebraterecovery.com.

15. A couple of fine resources are CWIVES (Christian Wives Initiating Valu-
ing Enjoying Sex), www.healthyrelationshipsrx.com/cwives/, *and Passion
Pursuit: What Kind of Love Are You Making?* by Linda Dillow and Dr. Juli
Slattery.

16. Adapted from https://www.authenticintimacy.com/resources/7026/ive-
never-prayed-about-sex-with-my-spouse-before-how-do-i-start.

17. Helen Kooiman Hosier, *100 Christian Women Who Changed the 20th Century*
(Grand Rapids: Revell, 2000), 350–51.

18. To read more about sacrifices in the Old Testament and their meaning, see
"Why did God require animal sacrifices in the Old Testament?" at https://
www.gotquestions.org/Old-Testament-sacrifices.html.

DISCUSSION GUIDE

Dear Leader,

This book is designed to be read alone or studied in a small group setting. While it's written with a female audience in mind, it is completely applicable for a couples small group setting, as well.

Whether you are a group of two or a hundred and two, the discussion questions for each chapter will guide your conversation. My hope is to give you the tools to lead a successful dialogue as your group reads this book together. If you don't know where to start, we've given you a template with which to work. If you are an experienced leader, the discussion questions can serve to enhance your own ideas.

Regardless of whether you meet in a living room or a church building, the most important aspect of gathering together is intentionally building relationships. You'll notice that each week has a consistent format for discussion. Each section serves a purpose in relationship building.

Connect
This is a lighthearted getting-to-know-you-let's "break the ice" kind of question. It gets everyone talking about their experiences and helps group members know they're not alone.

Dig Deep (20–45 minutes)

These questions are designed to facilitate discussion. The best groups are not led by leaders who like to hear themselves talk but rather by leaders who like to hear others talk. There's nothing for you to "teach"; that's what the book is for. Your job is to ask questions that help to drive the discussion and life application deeper. You'll also want to lead by example in answering the questions yourself.

If you are leading the discussion, you'll want to familiarize yourself ahead of time with the questions. As you read the chapter yourself, jot down additional questions you might present to the group. Make sure you pray for your group and for God's guidance as you lead the discussion.

Apply (5–10 minutes)

The "Apply" section is designed for personal reflection and then for goal setting. This helps the reader take all the information they've read and determine what one "nugget" they are going to own. This is the application to daily life that moves us to action. You can review these application suggestions, encouraging each group member to use them to apply what they're learning.

Pray

You can choose to have one person close in prayer or have a group prayer time. You can use the prayer included in the discussion guide or pray as you're led. Don't put undue pressure on yourself to be the perfect leader. It's far more important that you are an honest, authentic leader. Relax, trust God to lead you, share honestly, laugh, and have a good time discussing the book together.

The leader's guide is written so that you can meet and discuss one chapter a week. If you prefer a shorter study, you can easily discuss two chapters a week. If you do so, we recommend this schedule:

Week 1: Getting Started: The Roller Coaster of Emotions
Week 2: Chapters 1 and 2
Week 3: Chapters 3 and 4
Week 4: Chapters 5 and 6
Week 5: Chapters 7 and 8
Week 6: Chapters 9 and 10
Week 7: Chapters 11 and 12

To modify the leader's guide for a shorter study, choose whichever connect question you want to use, choose two "Dig Deep" questions from each chapter, and one "Apply" question. Close with your own prayer or combining the two prayers provided.

Enjoy learning from each other!

GETTING STARTED:
THE ROLLER COASTER OF EMOTIONS

Connect

Have everyone share with the group a little about themselves and where they are in their empty nest journey. When each person shares, have her choose one word she would use to describe her feelings about the empty nest. (Jot those words down—you'll want to review them at the end of the study.)

Dig Deep

1. The author shared that the reality of the empty nest grief didn't hit her until eight months after her youngest got married when everyone was talking about the back-to-school season. When and how has empty nest reality hit you?

2. What stinkin' thinkin' do you struggle with? (Are there any of the questions the author poses on page 20–21 [lens section] that you particularly resonate with?)

3. Looking at Satan's Lies and God's Replies on pages 23–25, which lies/replies do you need to use to get serious about tackling?

4. Did you make your own timeline like the author suggests on page 30? What did you discover about the years you have?

Apply

1. If you haven't already, think through the life audit questions that begin on page 31.

2. If you've already started thinking through those, was there anything that surprised you as it relates to what wisdom, experiences, passions, and talents you have to offer the world?

3. Choose at least one of the Satan's Lies and God's Replies that you'll focus on daily until we meet again. Put it as a wallpaper on your phone, write it on an index card and post it on your refrigerator, or write it on your bathroom mirror with a wet erase marker. Keep it in front of you so you can take next steps to get rid of that stinkin' thinkin' you don't want to carry around anymore!

Pray

Lord, thank You for bringing us together. Thank You for giving us this opportunity to explore this new season of life together. As we read and share, open each of our hearts up to what You want us to learn and where You want us to grow. More than anything, Lord, help us better come to understand how we are really better when we do life together with You. In Jesus' name, amen.

CHAPTER 1:
LET GO OF EXPECTATIONS

Connect

Word Association: When you think of parenting, what word comes to mind? Why?

Dig Deep

1. The author talks about feeling "left out" of her young adult's life. Can you relate to that feeling? Can you share a time where you've felt left out of your child's life?

2. Of the four parenting expectations we need to let go of mentioned in this chapter (expecting to know things, expecting their priorities to be the same as yours, expecting them to communicate with you like you want them to, and expecting to change them), which one do you struggle with the most? Why?

3. What is one thing you took away from this chapter or one *aha* you experienced?

4. Why is it so hard for us to respond to our adult child with, "I know he's trying to figure out life and I'm going to give him the space and the grace to do so"?

Apply

1. Pay attention to your disappointments this week. Whether it's in marriage, parenting, friendship, or even

in your work environment, it's likely that an expectation you had wasn't met. Try to rethink the situation removing the expectation.

2. The author says, "Straightforward, honest communication surrounded with love and grace will give your changing relationship its best opportunity." Pay attention to your communication this week. Commenting, complaining, or criticizing are not communicating. Guilt trips, sarcasm, or manipulating so things go like you want aren't either. Focus on straightforward, honest communication filled with love and grace in all your relationships.

Pray

Lord, letting go is hard! We know our young adults are finding their own way. We know they have to make mistakes and learn from them. We also know we have to let go and put them in Your hands. Help us grieve what isn't and accept what is, trusting that You're still at work and that You love them even more than we do. In Jesus' name, amen.

CHAPTER 2:
LET GO OF GUILT

Connect

Share a brief overview of your children's birth or adoption stories. (Length of labor, meds/no meds, how you came to adopt, something funny that happened, etc.)

Dig Deep

1. Too often we compare our insides to other people's outsides. Where do you tend to do that most? At church? At the grocery store? On social media? In your neighborhood?
2. The Perfection Infection fuels guilt. The author mentions five antidotes that stop the Perfection Infection. Which antidote do you need to focus on most (humility, confidence, grace, forgiveness, courage)? Why?
3. We have to let our young adult kids feel the consequences of their choices. Do you struggle with that at all? Why or why not?

Apply

1. If there's any area of your parenting where you need to forgive yourself or ask forgiveness from God, take time to do business with God this week. The minute you ask for forgiveness, it's given to you. God has too much for

you to do in this next season of life to be saddled with guilt!

2. Whichever antidote to the Perfection Infection you need to make progress on, take some specific steps this week to apply that to any real-life circumstances you might have responded to with guilt in the past. Use your antidotes to kick the Perfection Infection right out of your life.

Pray

Lord, we confess that too often we're saddled in guilt rather than walking free in grace. We know You don't expect perfection on this side of heaven. We know You see us through eyes of grace so help us let go of guilt. May we be women of humility, confidence, grace, forgiveness, and courage so we're emotionally and spiritually free for what You have for us in this exciting, next season of life. In Jesus' name, amen.

CHAPTER 3:
LET GO OF OPINIONS

Connect

Take a couple of minutes and share with the group your own experience of when you launched into adulthood.

Dig Deep

1. The author says that empty nest parents now belong to the "keep it shut" club. What do you find are the hardest things to "keep it shut" about?
2. "Pray, don't say." What is the hardest part of doing that?
3. The author says whatever our kids struggle with there are layers of struggle and no easy answers. Would you describe yourself as "safe" for your kids to be honest with? Do you respond or react? What's one way you'd like to grow to become more safe?

Apply

1. The author challenges us to live truth more than we speak truth. Brainstorm with the group practical ways to live truth.
2. Have someone read aloud Romans 12:9–21. What are some practical ways these verses show us how to love well?

Pray

Lord, we confess that we have opinions. We're also so used to leveraging our opinions in our kids' lives. However, we know it's time to let go of those. Give us compassion to see the layers of struggle in our kids' lives. Help us respond rather than react. More than anything, show us how to love well. In Jesus' name, amen.

CHAPTER 4:
LET GO OF TRADITIONS

Connect

What is your personal favorite Thanksgiving, Christmas, or other tradition?

Dig Deep

1. The author challenges us to separate the "what" and the "when" of traditions. Have you adjusted the timing of your holiday traditions to accommodate your kids' new families, adult status, or schedules? Was that hard or easy for you? Why?

2. Have you created any new empty nest traditions? Share any ideas you're thinking about establishing with the group.

3. What was the biggest takeaway you had in this chapter?

Apply (choose one or all)

1. Send out a "Christmas audit" to your family. Ask them to name their favorite holiday foods and traditions. If there's anything not mentioned, take it off your "to do" list!

2. Have someone read aloud Ecclesiastes 3:1. What does this verse tell us about change?

Pray

Lord, we confess that change is hard! We like things the way they've always been. Help us see that the only sure thing that never changes is You. You are the same yesterday, today, and tomorrow. Help us hold on loosely to our traditions. Show us how to be flexible with schedules and sensitive to the needs of our families. In Jesus' name, amen.

CHAPTER 5:
LET GO OF YOUR CHILD'S PROBLEMS

Connect

If you could have an unlimited supply of one thing for the rest of your life, what would it be?

Dig Deep

1. The author talks about the "messy middle" when our kids are adult age but not fully grown and no longer dependent upon us. Of the six guidelines mentioned on pages 95–97, which ones have you done in the messy middle? Which ones do you need to do?

2. Do you have a child who has said, "my life, my choice"? Of the realities mentioned on pages 99–101, which ones have you personally experienced?

3. Of the choices you as a parent now need to make, which one is the hardest for you to do (unconditionally love, not let this define your family, accept your child, find community, be grateful, help but not enable, or have unshakable faith)? Why?

Apply

Identify one thing you can affirm in each of your children. Communicate those this week in some way (text, email, in person, note in the mail, card for no reason, etc.).

Of the choices you now as a parent need to make, brainstorm with the group what one practical step you might take in making that choice happen.

Pray

Lord, letting go of our kids' problems is hard because we so badly want to help them! We're also used to helping them. When we're tempted to worry, convict us of our need to place our child in Your hands. When we're tempted to control, show us that You're working even when we don't see evidence of it. When we're tempted to enable, remind us that experiencing consequences is actually a gift. Help us to stay attached to our kids but detached from their problems. In Jesus' name, amen.

CHAPTER 6:
LET GO OF IDOLS

Connect

If you had the power of teleportation right now, where would you go and why?

Dig Deep

1. What was your biggest takeaway from this chapter? Were there any *aha* moments you can share with the group?
2. Of the idols mentioned in this chapter, which one do you struggle with the most? Why?
3. What are you most tempted to use to identify yourself (your address, your weight, your job or lack of job, your kids' choices, your choices, and so on)?

Apply

1. The author mentions four types of control on pages 120–126. Which one are you most characterized by? Brainstorm with the group different ways of responding so you can move away from control.
2. Take some time to clear out the clutter in your heart this week. Confess your idols to God, ask for His forgiveness, apologize for defining yourself by anything other than Him, receive His forgiveness, and walk in freedom.

Pray

Lord, thank You for this study. It's stretching and strengthening us. It's helping us look deep and clear out the clutter in our hearts that keep us from being all You want us to be. Reveal to us anything that we make more important than You. Lead us to walk in freedom and to be defined by You and You only. In Jesus' name, amen.

CHAPTER 7:
GRAB HOLD OF YOUR NEW MISSION FIELD

Connect

If you could give younger moms one piece of wisdom, what would it be? Why?

Dig Deep

1. What was your biggest takeaway from this chapter?
2. Who needs you? What "mission fields" mentioned in this chapter interest you the most? What do you most feel called to (other moms, youth, your kids' friends, neighbors and friends, grandkids)? Are there any mission fields not listed that you would add?
3. What was your kids' experience with grandparents? What do you want to emulate and what do you want to do differently?
4. The author says, "You are now extended family for your children and grandchildren." You may not have grandchildren yet, but have you considered the fact that once your child marries, they will now have a family they must consider ahead of you? Are you prepared for that reality? If you've already experienced that, what wisdom can you share with the group to make that transition?

Apply

1. Of the mission field that interests you the most, brainstorm with the group one practical next step you could take to explore that.
2. Begin praying this week about where God wants you to leverage your time, experience, and wisdom. Ask Him to connect the dots to the right opportunities.

Pray

Lord, we know You have something new for this season of life. Thank You for Your promises that You have a plan and a purpose for us! Help us see with Your eyes the needs around us. Show us the possibilities. Help us be in tune with Your Spirit so we can take the next right step to reach the mission fields around us. In Jesus' name, amen.

CHAPTER 8:
GRAB HOLD OF NEW PASSIONS

Connect

If you could do a two-day getaway with a friend, what would you do?

Dig Deep

1. The author talks about so many new opportunities available during the empty nest years. As you read this chapter, what were you most excited about?
2. Share with the group your "someday" that it's time to get serious about.
3. Do you feel you still have "nurturing" inside you? If so, what opportunities do you want to pursue that will allow you to still nurture in some way?

Apply

1. Share one thing on your "bucket list" or "someday" list you'd like to do. Brainstorm with the group one practical next step you could take to start working toward that goal.
2. Are there any nurturing opportunities you'd like to take action on (exchange programs, nursery worker, sponsor a child, Big Brothers Big Sisters, and such)? If so, share

that with the group to provide just a bit of accountability that you'll do something to move toward that.

Pray

Lord, there is so much possibility in this new era of our lives. Some of us have been so focused on our kids we've hardly had time to dream for ourselves. Help us connect to the passions You've created in us. Tune our heart to Yours to be more aware of the nurturing needs around us that we can meet. Keep growing excitement and anticipation in our hearts about what You have for us in these upcoming years. In Jesus' name, amen.

CHAPTER 9:
GRAB HOLD OF NEW FRIENDSHIPS

Connect

Share a two-minute version of your life story.

Dig Deep

1. What was your biggest takeaway from this chapter on friendship?
2. Have you ever been in an environment where you really felt like you belonged? Can you identify what relational elements made that happen?
3. Are you more of a "here I am" or a "there you are" person? Talk about practical ways we can each move more intentionally toward being a "there you are" person consistently in social situations.

Apply

1. Share a three-minute version of your faith story. After each person shares, have someone pray for her.
2. Share with the group two or three experiences you have had that you can offer to someone else.

Pray

Lord, You didn't do life alone on this earth. You modeled community and showed us what it looks like to do life with others. Help us be cheerleaders for one another. Show us when our story can help another mom who is experiencing something similar. Keep us aware of the lies of the enemy that want to keep us isolated and lonely. And thank You for Jesus leading the way in being a "there you are" person. May we continue to become more like Him every day. In Jesus' name, amen.

CHAPTER 10:
GRAB HOLD OF YOUR MARRIAGE

Connect

Where did you go on your honeymoon? (If you have any unmarried study members, ask them to share their favorite vacation spot.)

Dig Deep

1. What was your biggest takeaway from this chapter on marriage?
2. Of the self-reflection questions in the appendix, what are two pieces of "junk in the trunk" you probably need to deal with? Brainstorm with the group the next right step you can take on each of those.
3. Of the gaps mentioned in this chapter (the communication gap, the sex gap, the connecting emotionally gap, or the having fun gap), which one did you resonate with the most? Can you identify any other gaps you might be experiencing in your marriage?

Apply

1. Share what your favorite date night activity is with the group. If you're out of the habit of dating, ask the group to hold you accountable to get a date night on the calendar.

2. Pray for your husband every day this week. Pray for his hopes, dreams, struggles, and any way either of you are frustrated in your marriage.

Pray

Lord, thank You for marriage. We confess it's way harder than we ever thought it would be. Help us see our husbands through Your eyes. Where we need help, give us the courage to ask for it. Where we need to make effort, prompt us to engage. Where we need hope, let us borrow Your hope. More than anything, help us love well, even when it doesn't seem to be reciprocated. In Jesus' name, amen.

CHAPTER 11:
GRAB HOLD OF GOD'S HAND

Connect

The 60s, 70s, 80s, 90s: Which decade do you love the most and why?

Dig Deep

1. What was your biggest takeaway from this chapter on faith?
2. The author mentions several areas of our lives that we need to be stewarding (time, physical health, money). Which one do you need to get more serious about? Why do you think you've let that slide?
3. Where do you want to grow in your relationship with God? Talk with the group about ideas for how to do that.

Apply

1. If you don't already, get in the habit of praying before your feet hit the floor in the morning. Even if it's just, "Lord, it's a new day. Show me the way today." Share how you make prayer a part of your day.
2. Once of the most powerful prayers to pray is, "Lord, unself me." Talk about the implications of that prayer in our lives.

Pray

Lord, thank You for Jesus. Thank You for His sacrifice for us. Thank You for His human experience that showed us the way. We know You ask us to steward this life You've given us. Help us to keep running after You and Your transforming truth. In Jesus' name, amen.

CHAPTER 12:
YOUR ENCORE

Connect

What's your favorite movie or stage show? Why?

Dig Deep

1. What has been your biggest takeaway from this book?
2. The author has described the empty nest as parenthood retirement, the open nest, and the encore season of life. Which of those do you most resonate with? Do you have another way you like to describe it?
3. What word would you use now to describe your feelings about the empty nest? (Jot these words down as the group members share them.) Now compare them to the words used to describe everyone's feelings in week one. Have they changed?

Apply

1. What mom do you know who needs this book? Who can you bless with a copy? Share your plans with the group.
2. Get an "empty nest" girls' night out scheduled as a follow-up from this time together.

Pray

Lord, thank You for giving us the opportunity to spend this time together. Show us how to stay connected with You and each other. Help us let go of expectations, guilt, opinions, traditions, our child's problems, and the misplaced worship of idols of the heart. With our hands open, keep reminding us to hold on to our new mission field, our passions, our friendships, our marriage, and most importantly, Your hand. Keep the "full life" vision burning brightly in front of us. In Jesus' name, amen.

Author's Note:

If your group enjoyed *Empty Nest, Full Life* and would like to do another study, check out *No More Perfect Moms*, *Better Together*, and *No More Perfect Marriages*, which are also great studies for empty nest moms. You can find free video curriculum and more information at www.NoMorePerfect.JillSavage.org and www.BetterTogetherBook.JillSavage.org.

CONNECT WITH THE AUTHOR

Dear Reader,

I'd love to hear how this book has encouraged you personally! Let's connect online! If you want to keep the encouragement going, get on my VIP list so you'll receive inspiration in your inbox. (www.jillsavage.org/subscribe). And if you're looking for a speaker for your next event, you can request me as a speaker at www.jillsavage.org. I'd love to partner with you!

Email:	jill@jillsavage.org
Website/Blog:	www.JillSavage.org
Facebook:	@jillsavage.author
Twitter:	@jillsavage
Instagram:	@jillsavage.author

Make sure you check out www.EmptyNestBook.com for accompanying resources like the *Empty Nest, Full Life Journal*, as well as links to *Empty Nest, Full Life* retreats that will help you share what you've learned and keep the encouragement going!

Joining you in the journey,

Jill

MORE FROM JILL SAVAGE

No More Perfect Kids guides you in truly appreciating your kids. It will teach you how to study and become an expert on your children, because you cannot fully embrace them until you truly know them. You'll be inspired to apply the practical, realistic, and relevant ideas and tactics to your parenting.

978-0-8024-1152-5

Many marriages suffer for a lack of intimacy, but most couples don't know why. Jill and Mark Savage do, because it nearly ended their marriage before they realized it. In *No More Perfect Marriages*, they guide couples in discovering the Perfection Infection, rooting it out, and restoring trust and intimacy.

978-0-8024-1493-9

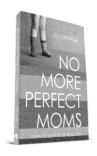

If you've ever forgotten to pick your kid up from soccer practice or accidentally worn two different shoes to the grocery store, read on. In favor of some much-needed realism and in a manner invitational of God's grace, author Jill Savage explains why she has set aside her visions of being a mother with a sparkling home who serves all her meals on fine china.

978-0-8024-0637-8

also available as eBooks

MOODY
Publishers®

*From the Word **to Life**®*

BEING A MOM IS HARD, BUT IT DOESN'T HAVE TO BE LONELY.

Mothering is hard work, but it's even harder when we go it alone. In *Better Together*, Jill Savage presents a vision of motherhood as a group effort. Walking moms through the ins-and-outs of building and maintaining a mom tribe, she shows how mothering is made easier—and more rewarding—when done together.

978-0-8024-1379-6　|　also available as an eBook

TIRED OF FEELING LIKE NO ONE UNDERSTANDS YOUR STRUGGLES AS A MOM? LOOK NO FURTHER.

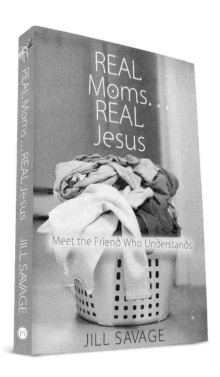

What does Jesus know about the peanut-butter-and-jelly life of a mom? Plenty, says Jill Savage. By exploring Jesus' human experiences on this earth, you will come to know the real Jesus—a friend who understands.

978-0-8024-8361-4 | also available as an eBook

WHAT AM I GOING TO DO WITH MY RETIREMENT?

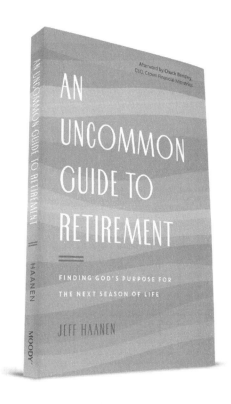

**MOODY
Publishers®**

From the Word to Life®

Learn how to discern God's purpose for your retirement by taking an uncommon approach. Jeff Haanen looks biblically and practically at the need for rest and purpose in retirement. And teaches you how to take a sabbatical rest in early retirement, rethink "work," understand family systems, and leave a legacy.

978-0-8024-1892-0 | also available as an eBook